T0246851

DENNIS YEN

SLURP

Recipes to Elevate Your Noodles

Photography by Lina Eidenberg Adamo

[T] tra.publishing

For many people, instant noodles are everyday saviors. You can come home from school or work tired and hungry, and in just ten minutes, you can have a bowl of noodles that hits the spot. Noodles and ramen have gained significant attention in recent years, with noodle shops popping up in many neighborhoods and a wide variety of noodle dishes intriguing both food enthusiasts and home cooks. However, for most people, instant noodles are still the only ones prepared at home. More complicated dishes, some with unfamiliar ingredients, are relatively uncharted territory and may feel daunting.

To me, noodles equate to home. I was raised on Chinese and Vietnamese cuisines, both of which are rich in diverse noodle dishes. With Slurp, I aim to usher you into the delightful world of noodles—a world teeming with possibilities. Bring this book into your kitchen and make it as essential as your cutting board. It contains noodle dishes for every occasion, from quick fifteen-minute bowls to more intricate recipes requiring hours of preparation (but not chef-level skills!). You'll also find recipes for flavorful broths and various sauces, allowing you to whip up noodles tailor-made to your palate and preferences.

My hope is, over time, you'll venture out and experiment with the delicious combinations this book offers. Who knows? You might discover a flavor pairing that makes your taste buds dance with every slurp. I hope you do.

Dennis Yen

FOOD
IN MY LIFE

~~~

I grew up in a large family with an immense passion for food and anything food-related. Whenever we talk over the phone or meet in person, the first question, in Cantonese, is always, "Have you eaten?" In my family, it's equivalent to asking, "How are you?" and how you feel at that moment depends on whether you've eaten or not. For instance, if it's late at night and you haven't eaten, immediate concern arises—"Why haven't you eaten? Is something wrong?" I've learned to always say "yes" to the question in order to avoid unnecessary worries.

My profound interest in food stems from my upbringing. I remember every weekend, a five-gallon (twenty-liter) pot simmered on the stove, the scent of its aromatic broth wafting through our home. As far back as I can recall, my mother always prepared a bountiful variety of noodles. One weekend it might be simple rice noodles with a savory chicken broth; another time, a rich beef broth with aromatic spices. But the best were the occasions she prepared the Vietnamese noodle dish, pho. Even today, every time I visit, my mother serves steaming bowls of noodles, with magical broths, every conceivable condiment, and a mountain of toppings. Her food is unparalleled; no matter what she serves, it tastes better than anything else I eat anywhere else.

While my love of food has its roots in my upbringing, it doesn't mean I always appreciated the fact that my family enjoyed different food than my friends' families. Growing up in a Western culture in Sweden, eating Asian food was considered peculiar and different. I used to feel embarrassed that we weren't like everyone else. "Why don't we ever eat meatballs, potatoes, and gravy with a glass of milk?" I wondered. Instead, we consumed dishes with fermented beans, fish sauce, and unfamiliar warm vegetables. But as I grew older, I began to cherish the meals my mother prepared. Today, noodles are trendy, and even fermented, sometimes "pungent," ingredients have their place.

For many years now, I've been proud of and grateful for the food culture I experienced as a child. It's largely shaped who I am today. Much of the food I prepare has its origins in Asian kitchens, drawing inspiration primarily from China, Vietnam, South Korea, Thailand, and Japan. Cooking ramen or other noodle dishes as an adult feels instinctive. I adore experimenting and trying new dishes as much as I relish the classics. To me, the food I cook is an expression of love and appreciation; it's a way to convey memories and narrate my family's history.

MY NOODLE PHILOSOPHY

I uphold a simple philosophy when I prepare noodle dishes: it shouldn't be complicated. Crafting a magical bowl of noodles should be as straightforward as boiling pasta or frying sausages. Like any culinary endeavor, creating dishes from scratch naturally takes more time. Personally, I cherish pasta with meat and tomato sauce, but I don't always make the sauce from scratch; oftentimes, I opt for the store-bought variety.

The same principle applies to noodles: you can choose to handcraft the noodles for your dishes, or you can purchase ready-made ones. Both versions have their unique charm. Like all facets of cooking, you get to decide how deeply you wish to immerse yourself in each ingredient. Many people believe that preparing ramen involves an exhaustive effort, leaving you almost drained by the time you're ready to serve. While there's some truth to this, it typically holds only if you choose to create everything from scratch and intend to consume the dish the same day. But, of course, there's a solution. True to my noodle philosophy, it shouldn't be complicated—it doesn't have to be a chore.

One helpful approach to finding a balance with noodle dish creation is to master one component at a time and purchase the rest. For example, you can start by mastering the craft of a kick-ass broth. Once you feel comfortable with this, you can then delve into making your own noodles, before moving on to another challenge.

A useful perspective is to view each noodle dish as a sum of its individual components. These can range from various types of noodles, broths, sauces, oils, toppings, and other accompaniments. Acquire a collection either by buying these ready-made or preparing them from scratch and storing them in your pantry, fridge, or freezer. Then, you're equipped to whip up any dish your heart desires. In my freezer, you'll find wontons and dumplings with varied fillings, broths, slow-cooked pork belly, and handcrafted noodles of different types—all poised to satiate any emerging cravings. My pantry is stocked with an assortment of oils, sauces, spice mixes, and condiments that can be ladled over any noodle. You get the idea. It's a luxury to have access to all these treasures, and the secret is foresight and preparation. Noodles should be simple. Why overcomplicate them?

HOW
TO USE
THIS BOOK

Slurp imposes no strict rules. Rather, my aim is to guide you—to be the compass steering your culinary journey toward mastering an array of delectable noodle dishes. One valuable tip, however, is to read through the entire recipe before starting. This ensures you have all the ingredients on hand and provides an overview of the workflow. Some ingredients might be unfamiliar to you: delve deeper on pages 18. Today, several established online retailers offer a vast array of Asian products. Curious about various noodles? Refer to page 14. There are also certain utensils that can facilitate the cooking process, which are outlined on the following page. You probably have most of them already, and if not, improvisation usually works wonders.

KITCHEN TOOLS

Mortar and Pestle

Kitchen Torch

Ladle

Mixer

Wok Pan

Kitchen Scale

Zester

Strainer

Peeler

Spatula

Pots

Soup Bowl

Skillet

Salt and Pepper Grinders

Rolling Pin

Knife

Measuring Cups

Chopsticks

Bowls

Tongs

Pasta Machine

Hand Strainer

Thermometer

Whisk

Juicer

Baking Dish

Garlic Press

DIFFERENT TYPES OF NOODLES, SHEETS, AND WRAPPERS

1. Glass Noodles
Thin and translucent, glass noodles are typically made from mung beans, although they can be made from tapioca and sweet potato. Glass noodles have a delightful texture and absorb liquids well. Thus, they're well-suited for salads with dressings. In this book, I use glass noodles for spring rolls.

2. Ramen Noodles
Available both fresh and dried, these noodles are crafted from wheat flour, salt, and water. Some brands contain kansui, an alkaline ingredient, in the dough (more on page 96), giving the noodles more elasticity (their trademark chewiness) and making them less absorbent in soups.

3. Wheat Noodles
Most commonly sold dried, wheat noodles come in various thicknesses and shapes. They're made from wheat flour, salt, and water, and some may contain eggs. I like kuan miao noodles, which are hand-cut. Wheat noodles work well in both stir-fries and soups.

4. Instant Noodles
There's a vast array of varieties. I've used both economical and pricier types, the distinction (beyond price) being that the costlier ones tend to have thicker noodles, and their accompanying seasoning is often richer in flavor. Instant noodles are a delicious and easy addition to soups.

5. Udon Noodles
Crafted from wheat flour, salt, and water, udon can be bought both fresh and dried. Fresh udon is chunkier and chewier, while dried udon is slimmer, with a smooth texture. Udon noodles are delightful in dishes both with and without broth.

6. Rice Noodles
Like wheat noodles, rice noodles come in various forms. They are made from rice flour, tapioca, salt, and water. Not particularly flavorful on their own, they are typically used in noodle dishes that have aromatic and potent spices. They're commonly found in salads, stir-fries, and soups.

7. Rice Paper
Rice paper, which is sold in sheets, is highly versatile and can change in texture based on the method of preparation. It's made from rice flour, tapioca, salt, and water. Like rice noodles, rice paper has a mild taste, making it suitable for dishes that are more robust in flavor.

8. Spring Roll Wrappers
The sheets I frequently use are made from wheat flour, salt, and water, and measure approximately 8 x 8 inches (20 x 20 cm). You can find them in stores' frozen sections, often labeled "spring roll pastry." There are also versions made from rice flour.

9. Wonton Wrappers
These are thin sheets of dough, usually square in shape, crafted from wheat flour, water, eggs, and salt. They are sold fresh or frozen, with a typical pack containing around sixty sheets.

10. Egg Noodles
Egg noodles are available in different sizes and made from wheat flour, water, eggs, and salt. These noodles are generally sold dried but can be found fresh in the refrigerated section of some Asian stores. They are delicious in stir-fries and soups.

TIPS ON NOODLE PREPARATION

Homemade Ramen Noodles

The cooking time for homemade ramen noodles varies depending on the thickness—thinner noodles cook faster. I typically prepare my noodles at thickness level four on my pasta machine and have learned that the cooking time for these is thirty seconds. But pasta machine settings can vary: the simplest way to determine the perfect cooking time for your specific noodles is to test cook a few. I boil my homemade ramen noodles similarly to regular wheat noodles: in a capacious pot of boiling water. After boiling, I drain the noodles and then rinse them carefully, to remove as much starch as possible. (If I'm using the noodles for cold dishes that aren't submerged in broth, I'll rinse them thoroughly with cold water to halt the cooking process as well as remove starch.)

Rice Noodles

Rice noodles demand a different approach than the usual boiling in a pot of water. Here's how to cook them:

Place the noodles in a large bowl. Boil a generous amount of water and pour it over the noodles (there should be enough water to cover the noodles), then cover the bowl. Let the noodles sit for ten to fifteen minutes, occasionally lifting the lid to gently separate the noodles if they are sticking together.

Taste a noodle or two as they begin to soften: you'll know they are done when they're flexible enough to wind around your finger and they have a pleasant al dente bite. Drain the noodles and rinse with cold water.

It's essential to note that rice noodles vary by brand and size, so soaking times may differ. The same process can be applied to glass noodles.

Wheat Noodles and Egg Noodles

Bring a large pot of water to a boil—to ensure even cooking, the noodles require ample space to move around. The instructions and timing on packaging are only approximate, so tasting is essential. A method my mother taught me is to take a few noodles out of the pot, rinse them with cold water, and sample to check the texture. They should be soft and fully cooked but not mushy. If you're uncertain, it's best to taste multiple times.

After cooking, drain the noodles and rinse them well with cold water. This stops the cooking and removes excess starch. This same approach applies to udon noodles and kuan miao.

PANTRY ESSENTIALS

〰

1. Aonori. Dried seaweed that's washed and chopped. It imparts a delightful sea flavor and is used as a topping or garnish.

2. Black Bean Sauce. Essential in Chinese cuisine, this sauce is composed of fermented black beans and soy. Great in stir-fries with noodles.

3. Chinkiang Vinegar (black rice vinegar). A staple in Chinese cuisine, it provides sweetness and acidity, and is excellent for sauces.

4. Coconut Milk. Consider buying coconut milk from Asian stores, where the brands tend to be richer, creamier, and more aromatic. My favorite brand is Aroy-D.

5. Doubanjiang (fermented fava beans). This key ingredient in many Sichuan dishes is made from fermented broad beans and chili peppers. It brings saltiness, umami, and a delightful heat.

6. Dried Mini Shrimp. A flavor enhancer often used in Asia, dried shrimp are delicious sautéed with garlic, ginger, and shallots, and are useful in soups, stews, and sauces.

7. Dried Shiitake Mushrooms. They offer a rich umami flavor. I use them in soups, sauces, or sliced in dishes.

8. Douchi. Sun-dried fermented black beans rich in umami. They create a complex and profound taste.

9. Fish Sauce. Crafted from fermented anchovies, salt, and water, fish sauce delivers a pronounced saltiness with an aromatic nature.

10. Gochujang. A Korean fermented chili paste with a potent and fruity chili taste that's slightly sweet and salty.

11. Katsuobushi (bonito flakes). The bonito fish is smoked and dried, then shaved into thin flakes, which are often utilized in Japanese cuisine, mainly in soups or as toppings.

12. Japanese mayonnaise. I prefer the Kewpie brand, which is made from egg yolk, apple, and malt vinegar, with a fresh and creamy flavor.

13. Laksa Paste. Bursting with aromatic spices and flavors. Freshen it up with lemongrass, ginger, onion, and chili peppers, and you have an excellent base for the noodle dish laksa.

14. Light and Dark Soy Sauce. Light soy sauce is salty, with a robust umami flavor, while dark soy sauce is less salty, with more color. They are not interchangeable, and the label usually specifies whether the soy sauce is light or dark. Tamari sauce can be substituted for soy sauce for those with gluten intolerance.

15. Mirin. Mirin is a Japanese fermented rice wine with low alcohol content. It delivers umami with a hint of sweetness.

16. MSG. A flavor enhancer representing the fifth basic taste, umami, MSG is used to elevate other flavors.

17. Oyster Sauce. Crafted from oyster extract, it's sweet and salty with a pronounced umami.

18. Palm Sugar. Frequently used in Thai cuisine, it has a stronger flavor than granulated sugar. Perfect for balancing heat.

19. Red and White Miso. Both are made from soybeans. The difference is that white miso is saltier and fermented with rice, while red miso is sweeter and fermented with barley.

20. Red Curry Paste. A classic Thai curry paste that, besides red chili peppers, includes lemongrass, kaffir lime leaves, and galangal. Commonly used in curries and soups.

21. Saké. An alcoholic rice wine made from polished rice that has been fermented. It's known for its sweetness and low acidity.

22. Sesame Oil. Buy the toasted variety, which has a more pronounced and robust sesame flavor. I recommend purchasing sesame oil from Asian stores.

23. Sesame Paste. Produced from toasted sesame seeds, this paste is a delightful flavor enhancer. I recommend buying it from Asian stores as their brands are usually smoother and creamier.

24. Shaoxing Wine. A Chinese rice wine used in numerous Chinese dishes, it heightens and deepens the flavor of any recipe.

25. Shrimp Paste in Soybean Oil. A delightful blend reminiscent of fermented fish sauce. It provides a deep flavor suitable for soups.

26. Sriracha. A spicy sauce made from chili peppers and flavored with roasted garlic, vinegar, salt, and sugar.

27. Tamarind Paste. Tamarind is a tropical fruit native to Africa but also heavily used in Southeast Asia. It's made into a paste, which provides a well-balanced blend of sweet and sour.

28. Tsuyu. Bottled liquid umami, derived from kombu (dried seaweed) and shiitake, that is used as a flavoring, primarily in soups. There are vegan versions and those that contain bonito.

29. Wood Ear Mushrooms. This type of mushroom is widely used in Chinese cooking. Sold dried, it offers minimal flavor, but introduces a crispy texture.

30. Yuzu Juice. Yuzu, grown in South Korea and Japan, is a cross between a lemon and a mandarin. It has a refreshing sour taste distinct from other citrus fruits.

THE IMPORTANCE OF MISE EN PLACE

We've all been there. You're rummaging through drawers and cabinets, swearing that just yesterday you saw that spice packet in the top drawer—or was it the middle one? Or perhaps you overlooked the second line of the recipe, which stated the onion needed to be sautéed before adding it to the soup. The fish you're preparing has been overcooked, and the sauce in the pot has burnt to a crisp. Everything's chaotic, and you ask yourself, "Why does this always happen?"

Of course, there's a solution to this chaos, and the answer is planning and preparation. Applying mise en place—a French term meaning "everything in its place"—is a well-used concept in kitchens and restaurants. It involves peeling, cutting, chopping and prepping ingredients and then organizing them within arm's reach. Mise en place is essential in professional kitchens. If you adapt this concept to your home kitchen and prepare thoroughly, you'll feel less rushed and can focus more on critical tasks, like cooking that fish perfectly.

When I cook, I always try to prep my ingredients when everyday life allows time for it. For me, cooking is calming and relaxing; I want to feel in control. Feeling stressed is the last thing I desire. I believe food prepared with care tastes so much better.

Some recipes in this book have multiple steps and might seem demanding at first glance. My best advice is to read through the recipe at least once before you get started. Ensure all tools and ingredients are ready, and do the necessary preparations before starting the actual cooking. When it comes to noodles, it's vital to be present during the cooking process, and timing is crucial. For instance, after placing the cooked noodles in bowls and pouring the hot broth, the toppings should be added promptly, and the dish served immediately—so be sure you have prepared the toppings before it's time to boil the noodles!

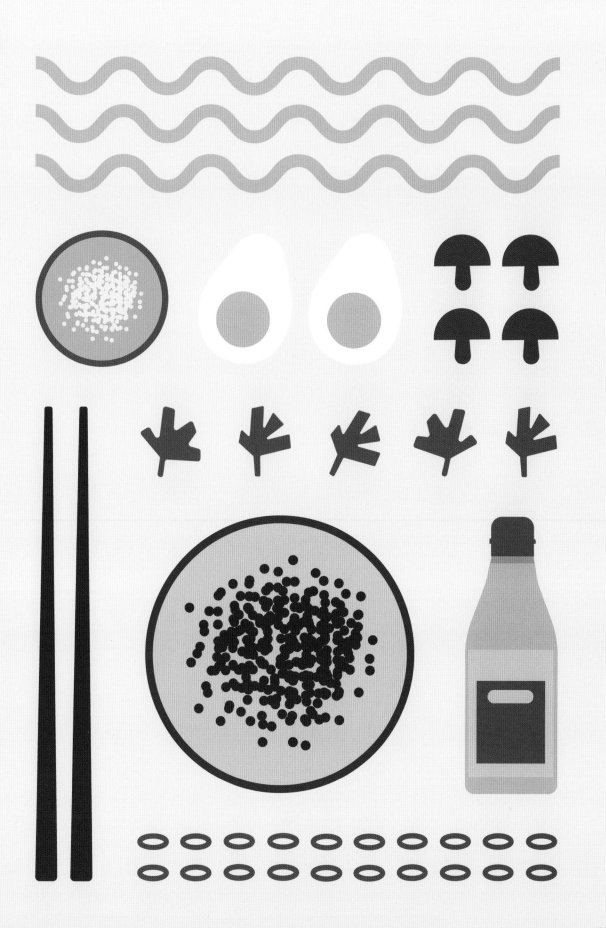

SAUCES AND SEASONINGS

In this chapter, I've gathered some of my absolute favorite condiments and sauces for the majority of dishes I prepare; they're especially great for noodle dishes. I strongly recommend making these sauces, rather than buying them, as they elevate the flavors of the recipes in this book. Moreover, they have a long shelf life, making them a superb foundation for any noodle dish you might want to prepare.

CRISPY
CHILI OIL

CRISPY
SHALLOT OIL

TERIYAKI SAUCE

SATÉ
SAUCE

XO SAUCE

Teriyaki Sauce

MAKES 2 ¾ CUPS (650 ML) 〜〜 10 MINUTES

This teriyaki sauce is an essential in my pantry. It's the shortcut to many dishes I make at home, and the best part is that it's incredibly simple to create. Use the sauce for marinating or in stir-fries, or reduce it for a thicker consistency. The sauce will last for 6 months in the fridge, but it'll likely be consumed before then.

INGREDIENTS:

1 cup (240 ml) light soy sauce
¾ cup (180 ml) mirin
¾ cup (180 ml) saké
⅓ cup (80 g) granulated sugar

INSTRUCTIONS:

1. In a medium saucepan over medium heat, combine the soy, mirin, saké, and sugar. Bring to a gentle simmer (do not let it boil). Stir until the sugar is completely dissolved.

2. Pour the teriyaki sauce into a clean glass jar and let it cool.

3. Seal the jar with an airtight lid and store in the refrigerator for up to 6 months.

Saté Sauce

MAKES ½ TO 1 CUP (120 TO 240 ML) 〜〜 45 MINUTES

This Vietnamese chili pepper-lemongrass sauce is brimming with delightful spicy, sweet, and salty flavors. Use it as a dipping sauce, in broths, for marinating, with noodles, or as you see fit. This somewhat forgotten sauce deserves more attention and must not be mistaken for the Indonesian peanut sauce, satay, which is pronounced the same.

INGREDIENTS:

2 lemongrass stalks
½ cup (120 ml) canola oil
2 large shallots, finely chopped
4 garlic cloves, finely chopped
4 large medium-hot red chili peppers, finely chopped
1 small hot red chili pepper, finely chopped
1 tablespoon red pepper flakes
3 tablespoons granulated sugar
2 tablespoons fish sauce
3 ½ tablespoons sriracha
Salt

INSTRUCTIONS:

1. Remove the outer layer of the lemongrass, trim off the hard root end, and finely chop the rest.

2. In a medium saucepan over low-medium heat, warm the oil, add the shallots, and sauté for 5 minutes. The oil should bubble slightly without browning the shallots. In intervals of 5 minutes each, add one ingredient at a time in the following sequence: lemongrass, garlic, and then the fresh chili peppers.

3. After an additional 5 minutes, add the red pepper flakes, sugar, and fish sauce. Allow the sauce to simmer gently for 2–3 minutes. Remove from heat, let cool, and stir in the sriracha. Season with salt to taste.

4. Store the sauce in a clean glass jar and seal tightly. Store in the refrigerator for up to 3 months.

XO Sauce

MAKES ABOUT 2 TO 2 ½ CUPS (500 TO 600 ML) 〰 1 HOUR (+ 45 MINUTES SOAKING TIME)

Dubbed the "Rolls-Royce of sauces," XO sauce has its origins in Hong Kong. While its name alludes to the luxurious XO cognac, the sauce doesn't actually contain any. Instead, many chefs associate the letters XO with luxury and premium quality. This sauce, with its intense and intricate flavors, is a veritable umami explosion. The recipe provided here is a simplified and accessible version, since some ingredients from the original recipe are costly and hard to come by outside of Asia. You can incorporate this sauce in various stir-fry dishes or as a delectable topping. You'll find countless reasons to reach for it. To ensure the XO's longevity, always use a clean spoon when taking sauce from the jar.

INGREDIENTS:

8 dried shiitake mushrooms
½ cup (120 ml) dried mini shrimp
½ cup (120 ml) Shaoxing
wine or saké, divided
1 ⅔ cups (400 ml) canola oil
3 ounces (80 g) prosciutto, shredded
or chopped into small pieces
4 large medium-hot red chili peppers,
seeds removed,
finely chopped
1 small hot red chili pepper, seeds
removed, finely chopped
2 tablespoons grated ginger
4 garlic cloves, finely chopped
¼ cup (60 ml) oyster sauce
1 tablespoon light soy sauce
1 tablespoon fish sauce
2 teaspoons granulated sugar
½ teaspoon freshly ground
white pepper
4 teaspoons Crispy Shallot Oil
(see page 28)
3 tablespoons red pepper flakes

INSTRUCTIONS:

1. Place the mushrooms and shrimp in separate bowls. Boil water and pour it over the mushrooms and shrimp to just cover them. Add 2 tablespoons of the wine to the shrimp bowl and mix gently. Let the mushrooms and shrimp soak for 45 minutes.

2. Strain the mushrooms and shrimp, reserving the liquid. Chop the shrimp and mushrooms separately and finely.

3. In a large pot (at least ½-gallon [2-l] capacity) over medium-high heat, heat the canola oil to about 230°F (110°C). The oil should fill the pot to a depth of about ¾ inch (2 cm). If you don't have a thermometer, you can test the oil by dipping a dry wooden chopstick into it: if the oil bubbles around the chopstick, it's hot enough.

4. Add the mushrooms to the oil and cook for 5 minutes, then add the shrimp and cook together with the mushrooms for an additional 10 minutes. Add the prosciutto and cook for 2 minutes. Use a slotted spoon to transfer everything from the oil to a bowl.

5. Add the chili peppers to the pot and sauté for 2 minutes. Add the ginger and sauté another 2 minutes. Add the garlic and cook for 1 minute, until it releases its aroma (don't let it brown). Scoop everything out of the oil and add it to the shrimp and mushroom mixture. Turn off the heat.

6. In a separate medium pot, combine the reserved mushroom and shrimp liquid, the remaining wine, and the oyster sauce, soy sauce, fish sauce, sugar, and pepper. Bring to a simmer and cook until the liquid has reduced by half. Stir in the shrimp-mushroom-chili mixture and then transfer everything to the pot with the oil. Heat over medium-high until it starts to bubble, then remove the pot from the heat and mix in the shallot oil and red pepper flakes.

7. Let the sauce cool, then pour it into to clean glass jars. Seal them well and store in the refrigerator for up to 6 months.

Crispy Shallot Oil

MAKES 1 ⅔ CUPS (400 ML) ⌇ 40 MINUTES

Of all the recipes in this book, this is undoubtedly the one I make the most. The reason is simple: the oil and shallots are so delicious, they complement everything. This condiment runs out in no time. Trust me, you'll wish you had doubled the batch from the start. Drizzle this aromatic oil, along with the crispy shallots, over your dishes to elevate any meal.

INGREDIENTS:

1 ⅔ cups (400 ml) canola oil
2 cups (250 g) shallots, thinly sliced
8 garlic cloves, thinly sliced

INSTRUCTIONS:

1. In a large pot over medium-high heat, heat the canola oil to about 230°F (110°C). If you don't have a thermometer, you can test the oil by dipping a dry wooden chopstick into it: if the oil bubbles around the chopstick, it's hot enough.

2. Add the shallots to the oil, and maintain a consistent heat.

3. Once the shallots begin to take on a bit of color (about 6 minutes), add the garlic, stirring occasionally with a heatproof spoon to prevent any shallots or garlic from sticking to the bottom.

4. Once the shallots and garlic have a light golden color, remove the pot from the heat and set aside to cool. (It's important to note that they will continue to cook from the residual heat, so remove the pot well before they turn brown. Be careful not to burn them. If you need to cool the garlic and shallots quickly, you can add a bit more oil or place the pot in a cold-water bath.)

5. Initially, the shallots might not seem very crispy, but they will become crispier as the oil cools. Once cooled, transfer the oil, shallots and garlic to a clean glass jar. Seal tightly and store in a cool place.

Crispy Chili Oil

MAKES ABOUT 2 CUPS (500 ML) ∿ 30 MINUTES

I warn you now, if there's anything one can become addicted to in the culinary realm, it's crispy chili oil (also known as chili crisp or chili crunch). As versatile as ketchup, this Asian equivalent is my go-to condiment for virtually everything. It employs the crispy shallot oil from the previous recipe for a result that is simply magical. Ideally, you'd use a thermometer for accuracy. You can adjust the spiciness by using different types of red pepper flakes. For a milder chili oil, I recommend pepper flakes made from Korean chili peppers. If you desire more heat, you can use pepper flakes from Thai chili peppers, or perhaps combine the two for a spiciness level that suits you best.

INGREDIENTS:

2 teaspoons Sichuan peppercorns
1 ½ teaspoons cumin seeds
2 ½ teaspoons fennel seeds
2 star anise pods
2 whole black cardamom pods
⅔ teaspoon whole cloves
2 tablespoons granulated sugar
1 tablespoon salt
1 ½ tablespoons MSG
1 ½ tablespoons red pepper flakes

2 cups (480 ml) canola oil
5 tablespoons red pepper flakes
3 tablespoons spice mixture (see above)
½ cup (120 ml) Crispy Shallot Oil
(see page 26)

INSTRUCTIONS:

1. Make the spice mixture: toast the Sichuan peppercorns, cumin, fennel, star anise, cardamom, and cloves in a dry skillet over medium-high heat for 3 minutes. Next, stir in the sugar, salt, MSG and first 1.5 tbs red pepper flakes.

2. In a small pot over medium-high heat, warm the canola oil to 310°F (155°C), then remove it from the heat and stir in the 5 tablespoons red pepper flakes. Let cool for 10 minutes, then stir in 3 tablespoons of the spice mixture.

3. Once the chili oil has cooled, mix in the shallot oil. Transfer the chili oil to clean glass jars, seal tightly, and store in the pantry for up to 2 months.

A 750–Square–Foot Asian Garden

One vivid memory from my childhood is the 750-square-foot garden plot my parents were fortunate to acquire after we moved to a quaint town in Sweden. Initially, the plot seemed rather ordinary. The soil hadn't been cultivated for years, and I remember the immense effort it took to clear everything and make the ground fertile and nutrient-rich again. I was still quite young, so I would accompany my parents to the garden, riding my tiny bike adorned with an orange flag and training wheels.

At that time, sourcing Asian vegetables in Sweden was a challenge. The most feasible solution was to grow our own, which is precisely what my parents did. They planted seeds of various vegetables they had brought and preserved from their homeland. In no time, our plot transformed into a verdant haven, boasting a variety of plants one could only dream of finding in our new home country.

I'd wander around curiously, tasting everything, asking questions, and developing a keen interest in the growing plants. My parents explained which vegetables and herbs complemented certain dishes and which dishes were incomplete without specific herbs. Their garden flourished and soon became the talk of the town. Many locals began visiting to purchase fresh produce for their families.

QUICK & EASY NOODLES

Not all heroes wear capes. The recipes in this chapter are perfect for rescuing you from ailments like brain fog, a rumbling stomach, or low spirits. Most of these delicious yet simple preparations use instant noodles to create sophisticated-tasting dishes that you can whip up when you're short on time, not in the mood to cook something elaborate, or just need a quick pick-me-up.

Saté Noodles with Crispy Green Onions

This is my take on a classic noodle dish from Shanghai. The oil used to cook the green onion becomes flavorful and aromatic. Combined with noodles, saté sauce, and a crispy topping, this dish is an incredibly delicious meal for any time of the day.

INGREDIENTS:

1 serving instant noodles
  (without the seasoning packet)
1 green onion
2 tablespoons canola oil, divided
Salt
1 garlic clove, pressed
1 tablespoon light soy sauce
1 teaspoon dark soy sauce
2 tablespoons Saté Sauce,
plus more for garnish (see page 26)

INSTRUCTIONS:

1. Cook the noodles (without the seasoning packet) according to the package instructions or until al dente. Drain and rinse with cold water.

2. Trim the ends of the green onion, and cut it crosswise into a green part and a white part. Julienne each part lengthwise into thin strips.

3. In a medium skillet over medium heat, warm 1 tablespoon of the oil, add the white part of the green onion, and fry until crispy and golden. Remove the onion from the pan using a slotted spoon, drain on a paper towel and sprinkle with salt to taste. Add the remaining 1 tablespoon of oil to the pan and add the green part of the onion. It will cook faster than the white part; ensure it doesn't burn. Remove with a slotted spoon, drain on a paper towel, and sprinkle with salt to taste.

4. Reduce the heat to low, add the garlic and sauté for a few seconds. Before it browns, add the light and dark soy sauce, followed by the saté sauce. Add the noodles into the skillet and mix with the sauce. Serve in a bowl, topped with the crispy onions and additional saté sauce, if desired.

Noodles with XO Sauce and Eggs

Nothing beats mixing noodles with a luxurious XO sauce brimming with umami and flavors. Imagine Beauty meeting the Beast, where the noodles play the Beast and the sauce is the Beauty. All's well that ends well, and they live happily ever after. Just as you will, once you discover this dish.

INGREDIENTS:

2 large eggs
Salt and freshly ground black
  pepper
2 tablespoons canola oil, divided
1 serving instant noodles
  (without the seasoning packet)
1 tablespoon light soy sauce
3 tablespoons XO Sauce
  (see page 27)
¼ cup finely chopped green onions,
  for garnish

INSTRUCTIONS:

1. In a bowl, whisk the eggs with a pinch each of salt and pepper.

2. In a small skillet over low heat, warm 1 tablespoon of the oil and add the eggs. Once they begin to set, gently stir with a spatula to form larger curds. Once the eggs are scrambled, transfer them to a bowl.

3. Cook the noodles (without the seasoning packet) according to the package instructions or until al dente. Drain and rinse with cold water.

4. In a medium skillet over medium-high heat, warm the remaining 1 tablespoon oil. Add the noodles, soy sauce, and XO sauce, and mix well. Sauté for 1 minute, then fold in the eggs.

5. Serve on a plate or in a bowl, topped with freshly ground pepper and green onions.

Noodles with Miso and Coconut Milk

I frequently enjoyed this delightful dish during my college days. The coconut milk lends the broth a creamy consistency, while the miso adds depth. The zing from the ginger pairs seamlessly with these flavors, resulting in a luxurious student lunch that's hard to top.

INGREDIENTS:

1 ¼ cups (300 ml) Mom's Chicken
  Broth (see page 127) or ½ bouillon
  cube dissolved in 1 ¼ cups
  (300 ml) water
½ cup (120 ml) coconut milk
1 tablespoon white miso
½ yellow onion, sliced
1 garlic clove, pressed
½ tablespoon finely julienned ginger
2 shiitake mushrooms, sliced
1 serving instant noodles
  (without the seasoning packet)
3 bok choy leaves, rinsed
¼ cup (26 g) finely chopped green
  onions, for garnish
Freshly ground black pepper

INSTRUCTIONS:

1. In a saucepan over medium heat, bring the broth to a boil. Add the coconut milk, miso, onion, garlic, ginger, and mushrooms. Reduce the heat to low, and simmer for 5 minutes.

2. In a separate pot of water, cook the noodles (without the seasoning packet) according to the package instructions or until al dente. In the last minute of cooking, add the bok choy leaves to the pot with the noodles. Drain the noodles and greens and transfer to a bowl.

3. Pour the broth mixture over the noodles and greens. Top with green onions and a few grinds of pepper.

Tangy Spicy Quick Noodles

The marriage of tang and heat is an Asian flavor pairing loved by many, and this noodle dish, using the broth flavor of your choice, delivers exactly that. Once you take that first savory slurp, you'll be completely engrossed. The world can wait; it's just you and the bowl.

INGREDIENTS:

1 serving instant noodles with seasoning packet (flavor of your choice)
3 iceberg lettuce leaves, rinsed and torn in half
2 tablespoons Chinkiang vinegar (black rice vinegar)
2 tablespoons Crispy Chili Oil (see page 29)
1 tablespoon light soy sauce
½ tablespoon toasted sesame oil
1 tablespoon chopped green onions
1 tablespoon chopped cilantro
1 tablespoon Crispy Shallot Oil (see page 28)
Freshly ground black pepper

INSTRUCTIONS:

1. In a saucepan, bring 2 cups (500 ml) of water to a boil. Add the noodles and the seasoning packet. Cook according to the package instructions or until al dente. In the last minute of cooking, add the lettuce leaves to the saucepan.

2. While noodles cook, in a large bowl, combine the Chinkiang, chili oil, soy sauce, and sesame oil. Add the cooked noodles, lettuce, and the broth they were cooked in. Top with green onions, cilantro, shallot oil, and a generous amount of pepper, to taste.

Noodles with Tomato and Egg

Fan ke chau tan is a classic dish from Chinese cuisine. Straightforward, quick to prepare, and budget-friendly, every family boasts its own unique version. It's typically served with freshly steamed rice, but I find it equally delicious nestled in a steaming bowl of soup with noodles.

INGREDIENTS:

1 serving instant noodles with
  seasoning packet (flavor of
  your choice)
1 tablespoon canola oil
1 garlic clove, finely chopped
1 green onion, chopped, divided
  into green and white parts
1 medium tomato, cut into wedges
1 tablespoon light soy sauce
½ tablespoon toasted sesame oil
Salt
1 large egg
1 tablespoon Crispy Shallot Oil
  (see page 28)

INSTRUCTIONS:

1. Set the noodle seasoning packet aside for later use. Cook the noodles according to package instructions or until al dente. Drain and rinse under cold water.

2. In a saucepan over medium heat, warm the canola oil. Add garlic and the white part of the green onion and sauté for 1 minute. Add tomato wedges and cook for a few minutes until they soften and the oil takes on a reddish hue.

3. Pour in 1 ⅔ cups (400 ml) water and add the seasoning packet, soy sauce, and sesame oil. Cover the pan and bring to a simmer. Simmer for 2–3 minutes, then season with salt to taste.

4. In the last minute of simmering, whisk the egg in a small bowl. Remove the lid from the saucepan and gently stir the broth in a circular motion with a spoon. Carefully pour the beaten egg into the soup. Once the egg begins to set, turn off the heat.

5. Transfer the noodles to a bowl, ladle the contents of the saucepan over them, and garnish with the remaining green onions and shallot oil.

Kewpie Mayo Noodles

In Japan, pairing ramen with mayonnaise is not uncommon: some find the soup reminiscent of a rich tonkotsu, while others liken it to a soupy carbonara. This recipe effortlessly transforms an otherwise simple instant noodle soup into a richer, creamier delight.

INGREDIENTS:

1 serving instant noodles
  with seasoning packet
  (flavor of your choice)
2 large eggs, divided
2 tablespoons Kewpie mayonnaise
½ garlic clove, grated

3 mushrooms, sliced
1 teaspoon butter
3 slices bacon
3 tablespoons finely chopped
  green onions
1 teaspoon toasted sesame seeds

INSTRUCTIONS:

1. Remove the seasoning packet from the instant noodles. In a serving bowl, whisk together 1 egg, the mayonnaise, garlic, and the seasoning packet.

2. Fill a small saucepan with water and bring it to a boil over high heat. Add the remaining egg (in its shell), reduce the heat to medium, and boil for 7 minutes. While egg cooks, prepare a bowl of ice water. Remove the egg from the water with a slotted spoon and transfer it to the ice water. Let it chill for 5 minutes, then carefully peel the egg and cut it in half lengthwise.

3. In a medium skillet over medium heat, melt the butter and sauté the mushrooms until golden brown. Remove the mushrooms from the heat and set aside. In the same skillet over medium heat, fry the bacon until slightly crispy, then drain on paper towels.

4. In a small saucepan, bring 1 ⅔ cups (400 ml) water to a boil. Add the noodles and cook as per the package instructions or until al dente. Strain the noodles, retaining the liquid.

5. Gently whisk the noodle water into the mayonnaise mixture. Mix in the noodles until coated and top with the halved egg, mushrooms, bacon, green onions, and sesame seeds.

Tofu Noodles

Perfect for warm days when you crave something cool and easy to prepare. Blended silken tofu coats the noodles, lending creaminess to the dish. Add flavor enhancers like tsuyu and sesame oil, paired with a few other simple ingredients, and you may discover a new summer favorite. This recipe is completely vegan.

INGREDIENTS:

1 serving instant noodles
  (without the seasoning packet)
7 ounces silken tofu
Salt
Granulated sugar
3 tablespoons light soy sauce
1 ½ tablespoons vegan tsuyu
1 tablespoon grated ginger
1 tablespoon toasted sesame oil
2 tablespoons finely chopped green
  onions
Freshly ground black pepper

INSTRUCTIONS:

1. Cook the noodles (without the seasoning packet) as per the package instructions or until al dente. Drain and rinse with cold water, and transfer to a serving bowl.

2. Pat the tofu dry with paper towels and place it in a blender. Add a pinch each of salt and sugar, and blend until the tofu becomes smooth, resembling a thick mayonnaise.

3. Add the tofu mixture to the bowl with the noodles. In another bowl, whisk together the soy sauce, tsuyu, and ginger. Pour the soy sauce mixture over the noodles, then top with sesame oil and green onions. Add pepper to taste, and stir to combine.

Cheddar Cheese Noodles

This noodle dish feels almost too simple to be included in this book, and I'm not even sure it qualifies as a recipe. But I must share it because the minimal ingredients combine to create a flavor that is surprisingly delicious. Cheese, eggs, and noodles— what's not to love?

INGREDIENTS:

1 serving instant noodles
  with seasoning packet
1 large egg
2 slices cheddar cheese
2 tablespoons finely
  chopped green onions

INSTRUCTIONS:

1. In a small saucepan, bring 1 ⅔ cups (400 ml) water to a boil. Add the noodles and seasoning packet and cook as per the package instructions or until al dente.

2. In the last minute of simmering, whisk the egg in a small bowl. Remove the lid from the saucepan and gently stir the broth in a circular motion with a spoon. Carefully pour the beaten egg into the soup. Once the egg begins to set, turn off the heat.

3. Pour the contents of the saucepan into a serving bowl and top with the cheese and green onions. Allow the cheese to become melty before digging in.

Noodles with Black Bean Sauce

I have a profound love for fermented foods, and fermented beans (found in black bean sauce) hold a special place in my heart. They add incredible standout flavor. Perhaps I adore them so much because my mother used fermented beans in many of her dishes during my childhood. The flavors of home are sometimes what I miss most, and this dish provides just that: a reminder of the taste of home.

INGREDIENTS:

⅓ cup (80 ml) finely chopped dried mini shrimp

3 tablespoons canola oil

2 green onions, finely chopped and separated into white and green parts

2 shallots, finely chopped

2 garlic cloves, finely chopped

6 shiitake mushrooms, sliced

3 tablespoons black bean sauce

8 ounces (250 g) dried wheat noodles

4 tablespoons Crispy Shallot Oil (see page 28)

¾ cup (180 ml) finely chopped cilantro

½ cup (100 ml) fried onions

Freshly ground black pepper

INSTRUCTIONS:

1. Fill a small bowl with water, add the shrimp, and let soak for 20 minutes. Drain and finely chop the shrimp.

2. In a medium skillet over medium-high heat, warm the canola oil. Add the white part of the green onions, and the shallots, garlic, and mushrooms, and sauté for 2 minutes. Be careful not to let them burn.

3. Add the shrimp and black bean sauce, and sauté for an additional 2 minutes. Pour in ¼ cup (60 ml) water and simmer for 2 minutes. Remove from the heat.

4. Separately, cook the noodles as instructed on the package or until al dente. Drain and divide between 4 serving bowls. Divide the sauce between the 4 bowls, and top each with 1 tablespoon of the shallot oil. Mix well, and top with the remaining green onions and the cilantro and fried onions. Add pepper to taste.

Kuan Miao Noodles with Teriyaki Beef and Bok Choy

Have you made the teriyaki sauce from the first chapter? Great! You can use it in this simple and quick recipe. I chose ground beef for this, but any protein will work. The noodles are tossed in a reduced teriyaki sauce for a perfect balance of sweetness, saltiness, and creaminess. Kewpie mayonnaise is also a delicious addition.

INGREDIENTS:

4 ounces (180 g) kuan miao noodles
1 head bok choy, sliced lengthwise
2 tablespoons canola oil
½ yellow onion, sliced
1 garlic clove, finely chopped
1 tablespoon grated ginger
3 ½ ounces (100 g) ground beef
¼ cup (60 ml) Teriyaki Sauce
  (see page 26)
1 tablespoon Chinkiang vinegar
  (black rice vinegar)
Freshly ground black pepper
Kewpie mayonnaise, for garnish
  (optional)

INSTRUCTIONS:

1. Fill a medium pot with water and bring to a boil. Add the bok choy and cook for 1 minute. Remove with a slotted spoon and set aside.

2. In the same pot, cook the noodles as instructed on the package or until al dente. Drain and rinse with cold water.

3. In a large skillet over medium-high heat, warm the canola oil. Add the onion, garlic, and ginger, and sauté for a few minutes. Add the beef, and cook, stirring, until the beef is browned. Pour in the teriyaki sauce and Chinkiang, and reduce the heat to medium-low. Simmer until the sauce is slightly reduced and thicker in consistency.

4. Stir in the noodles. Divide into two bowls and top each bowl with one piece of the bok choy. Garnish generously with pepper to taste, and drizzle with Kewpie mayonnaise if desired.

FRESH HERBS

GREEN ONIONS

Available in bundles at grocery stores, green onions possess a milder onion flavor. They are used both raw and cooked, in dishes like broths and stir-fries, and as toppings.

CILANTRO

This herb's taste can be described as slightly grassy, with a distinctive aromatic flavor. It's most often used as a topping or garnish. In my opinion, the world would be a dimmer place without cilantro; I can eat it on everything.

THAI BASIL

This herb is a fantastic flavor enhancer, slightly sweet and spicy, with undertones of licorice. It pairs well with dishes infused with the flavors of soy, lemon, and garlic. The leaves are best when fresh, so add them just before serving.

BEAN SPROUTS

Mung bean sprouts are a classic ingredient, commonly found in many Asian cuisines. Their flavor is delicate and reminiscent of snap peas, with a crisp texture. They can be enjoyed both cooked and raw.

BOK CHOY

This vegetable belongs to the cabbage family; it has dark green leaves and crispy white stems. Its taste melds the flavors of cabbage and spinach. Young bok choy can be eaten raw but is at its best when quickly cooked.

MEXICAN CORIANDER

This herb is reminiscent of cilantro but has a more intense flavor profile with hints of citrus and grass. It is a staple in Vietnamese cuisine, offering a refreshing touch and balancing dishes that might otherwise be overpowering, like those with sharp fermented flavors.

A Memory of Food

Which Cucumber Is the Crispiest?

~~~

When I was young, my parents always drilled my siblings and me on selecting the best ingredients in the grocery store. It was a routine every time we wandered around the produce or meat sections. From determining which lemons had the thinnest skin and thus more pulp to finding the crispiest cucumber or knowing a pork belly is at its best when the piece you purchase has at least three distinct layers of fat and meat: what used to be constant nagging has now transformed into a wealth of knowledge that I carry with me every time I shop. Sometimes, I find myself spending a considerable amount of time among the lemons to find the best one, wondering what others might think as they watch me meticulously pick up, compare, and put back lemons— after all, isn't one lemon just like any other?

~~~

NO-BROTH NOODLES

In this chapter, you will find noodle dishes without broth—they're ideal for those moments when you don't have the time or energy to make a broth but you still crave delicious noodles. These recipes, with slightly longer preparation times than the previous chapter's, encompass both classic and somewhat less traditional dishes. Once you include flavorful sauces and condiments, any of these noodle bowls is bound to be a hit.

Beef Chow Fun

Beef chow fun is an incredibly popular Cantonese wok dish. Every time I find it on a restaurant menu, I'm filled with joy. Wide rice noodles are stir-fried in a hot wok along with a delicious sauce, tender and juicy beef, and crisp bean sprouts. It's easiest to slice the beef if it's semi-frozen, so I recommend you plan ahead and place the meat in the freezer for two hours before working with it. I also like to soak the sliced meat before cooking it to draw out the myoglobin (the protein that makes the meat red)—the soaking makes the meat tastier and easier to cook.

INGREDIENTS:

10 ½ ounces (300 g) flank steak, preferably semi-frozen
1 pound (450–500 g) wide rice noodles
1 ¼ cups (300 ml) bean sprouts
3 green onions
4 tablespoons canola oil, divided
½ yellow onion, sliced
1 teaspoon toasted sesame oil
Freshly ground black pepper

Marinade:
1 teaspoon baking powder
1 tablespoon cornstarch
1 tablespoon oyster sauce
1 tablespoon light soy sauce
½ teaspoon freshly ground white pepper
1 teaspoon Shaoxing wine, saké, or other cooking wine
1 teaspoon granulated sugar
1 tablespoon canola oil

Sauce:
1 tablespoon light soy sauce
1 tablespoon oyster sauce

INSTRUCTIONS:

1. Slice the flank steak into thin strips.

2. Fill a large bowl with lukewarm water and add the sliced meat. Let soak for 15 minutes, then drain.

3. Place the noodles in a large bowl. Boil a generous amount of water and pour it over the noodles (there should be enough water to cover the noodles), then cover the bowl. Let the noodles sit for 10–15 minutes, occasionally lifting the lid to gently separate the noodles if they are sticking together. Taste a noodle or two as they begin to soften: you'll know they are done when they're flexible enough to wind around your finger and they have a pleasant al dente bite. Drain the noodles and rinse with cold water.

4. Rinse and drain the bean sprouts. Cut the green onions into three parts: one white and two green sections. Cut the white parts in half lengthwise.

5. Make the marinade: in a large bowl, combine the baking powder, cornstarch, oyster sauce, soy sauce, white pepper, wine, sugar, and canola oil. Add 2 tablespoons of water and stir until the sugar dissolves. Add the meat, stir to coat, and marinate for 5 minutes.

6. Make the sauce: in a small bowl, combine the soy sauce and oyster sauce.

7. Place a wok over high heat, and when the pan is very hot, add 3 tablespoons of the canola oil and then add the meat. Fry for 1 minute, stirring, then remove meat from the pan and place in a bowl.

8. Pour the remaining 1 tablespoon of canola oil into the wok and add the yellow onion and the white part of the green onions. Fry for 30 seconds on high heat. Add the noodles, stirring them gently so they don't break (a pair of chopsticks in each hand is a handy tool for stirring). Sauté the noodles for 2 minutes, then add the sauce and cook for 1 more minute. Add the green part of the onions and the bean sprouts and cook for 30 seconds.

9. Return the meat to the wok and cook for 1 minute. Turn off the heat and add the sesame oil. Divide the meat and noodles between 4 dishes and add black pepper to taste.

Yakisoba

This dish was my hero countless times during my student years, when I was often broke, hungover, and hungry. It's incredibly easy to make, and there's no right or wrong when it comes to the accompaniments: it's an ideal chance for a fridge cleanup. Use available noodles and accompaniments, add the simple sauce, and top with a fried egg and whatever else you crave.

INGREDIENTS:

6 dried shiitake mushrooms
4 lettuce leaves
8 ounces (250 g) egg noodles
1 tablespoon toasted sesame oil
2 tablespoons light soy sauce
1 tablespoon dark soy sauce
1 tablespoon oyster sauce
1 tablespoon 39 saké
  (or other cooking wine)
1 tablespoon fish sauce
4 tablespoons canola oil, divided
½ yellow onion, sliced
2 garlic cloves, sliced
4 large eggs
Katsuobushi (bonito flakes), for garnish
Aonori (dried seaweed) or seaweed
  chips, for garnish
Freshly ground black pepper, for
  garnish

INSTRUCTIONS:

1. Place the mushrooms in a small bowl and pour in enough water to cover them. Soak for 30 minutes, then remove the mushrooms and set them aside (keep the soaking liquid). Cut the lettuce leaves lengthwise down the middle and crosswise into 1-inch (3-cm) strips. Rinse them and set aside.

2. Cook the noodles as instructed on the package or until they are al dente. Drain and rinse with cold water.

3. Make the sauce: in a medium bowl, combine the sesame oil, both soy sauces, oyster sauce, saké, and fish sauce. Add ¼ cup (60 ml) of the mushroom liquid, and stir to mix. Slice the mushrooms.

4. In a wok over medium-high heat, warm 3 tablespoons of the canola oil. Add the onion and garlic and fry for 2 minutes, then add the mushrooms and lettuce and fry for another 2 minutes. Add the noodles and fry everything for 2 more minutes. Try to get some sear on the noodles and other ingredients as this adds a good flavor, but be careful not to burn them.

5. Once the ingredients in the pan have a nice color and some seared surface, reduce the heat to low and pour in the sauce. Stir to blend, and cook for 1 minute, until the sauce has reduced slightly.

6. In a large skillet over medium heat, warm the remaining 1 tablespoon canola oil, and fry the eggs. Divide the noodles between 4 bowls, top each with a fried egg, and garnish with katsuobushi, aonori, and pepper to taste.

Crispy Chinkiang Rolls

I stumbled upon these rolls by sheer coincidence, not realizing that after being cooked, rice sheets transform from sheets to rolls. To my surprise, in their new form, they became a perfect vehicle for sauce and accompaniments. The potent flavor of fermented beans combined with aromatic sauces like doubanjiang and crispy chili oil makes this dish both tasty and fun to eat.

INGREDIENTS:

5 tablespoons douchi
 (fermented beans)
1 (8-ounce/250 g) packet rice sheets
2 tablespoons canola oil
2 green onions, finely chopped and
 separated into white and green parts
2 garlic cloves, minced
4 tablespoons Crispy Chili Oil
 (see page 29)
1 tablespoon doubanjiang
 (fermented fava beans)
3 tablespoons Shaoxing wine or saké
½ cucumber, finely julienned
½ cup (100 ml) fried onion

Sauce:
3 tablespoons Crispy Chili Oil, plus
 more for garnish (see page 29)
2 tablespoons Crispy Shallot Oil
 (see page 28)
2 tablespoons light soy sauce
2 teaspoons toasted sesame oil
1 tablespoon Chinkiang vinegar
 (black rice vinegar)

INSTRUCTIONS:

1. Soak the douchi in lukewarm water for 1 hour. Drain the water and mash the beans with a fork.

2. Bring a large pot of water to a boil. Add the rice sheets and boil for 4–5 minutes or until they are al dente, then drain. The sheets will have curled up. Rinse them with plenty of cold water to remove starch and prevent them from sticking. Separate any sheets that have stuck together. Transfer the rolls to a large bowl.

3. In a medium skillet over medium-high heat, warm the canola oil and add the white part of the green onions, the garlic, and douchi, and sauté for 20 seconds to release the aromas. Add the chili oil, doubanjiang, and wine. Sauté for 1 more minute. Add the mixture to the bowl with the rolls and mix well.

4. Make the sauce: in a medium bowl, combine the chili oil, shallot oil, soy sauce, sesame oil, and Chinkiang. Pour this sauce over the rice rolls, add the cucumber, and mix well.

5. Divide the rolls between 4 bowls and top with the remaining green onions, fried onions, and more chili oil, if desired.

Mapo Tofu Mian

Mapo tofu is one of China's most celebrated dishes, known for its tingling sensation from Sichuan pepper, often described in Mandarin as málà, meaning "numbingly spicy." But fear not! With the right balance of málà and other rich flavors, you'll be compelled to savor every bite. This recipe is traditionally paired with rice, but I've tweaked it to be equally delightful with noodles.

INGREDIENTS:

2 tablespoons douchi
(fermented beans)
1 teaspoon salt, plus more for
 seasoning
About 1 pound (500 g) firm tofu,
 cut into ¾-inch (2-cm) cubes
2 tablespoons Sichuan pepper
4 tablespoons canola oil, divided
½ pound (250 g) ground beef
¼ cup doubanjiang
(fermented fava beans)
4 garlic cloves, finely chopped
1 tablespoon finely chopped ginger
6 green onions, trimmed, cut into
 2-inch pieces
Granulated sugar
1 teaspoon cornstarch
½ cup (125 g) wheat noodles
½ cup (25 g) finely chopped cilantro
Freshly ground black pepper

INSTRUCTIONS:

1. Fill a small bowl with water; add the douchi and let soak for 1 hour. Drain.

2. In a medium pot over medium heat, bring 3 ⅓ cups (800 ml) water and 1 teaspoon salt to a gentle simmer. Add tofu and simmer 15 minutes, lowering the heat as necessary to maintain a simmer. Remove the tofu from the water with a slotted spoon and set aside to drain on paper towels.

3. In a small dry skillet over low-medium heat, toast the Sichuan pepper for 1–2 minutes. Let cool slightly, then grind the pepper coarsely using a spice grinder or mortar and pestle.

4. In a wok or deep skillet over medium-high heat, warm 2 tablespoons of the oil. Add the ground beef and 1 tablespoon of the Sichuan pepper and sauté until browned. Transfer beef to a bowl.

5. Add the remaining oil to the wok. Stir in the doubanjiang until the oil takes on a red hue. Add the douchi, garlic, and ginger and sauté for 1 minute.

6. Add the tofu and 1 ⅔ cups (400 ml) water to the wok. Stir gently to avoid breaking the tofu. Once the mixture is simmering, return the beef to the wok, along with the green onions. Cook for 5 minutes or until the scallions soften slightly. Season with salt and sugar to taste. If overly salty, balance with more sugar.

7. In a small bowl, combine the cornstarch and 2 tablespoons water. Gradually stir this mixture into the wok until the sauce thickens—it should be neither watery nor too dense.

8. Cook noodles as per package instructions or until al dente. Drain and divide between 4 bowls. Top with your desired amount of tofu. Garnish with cilantro, black pepper, and extra Sichuan pepper for added kick, if desired.

HOW TO FOLD WONTONS

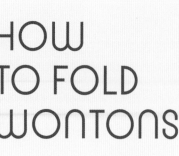

Step 1:
Lay out your filling, wonton wrappers, and a bowl of water on a work surface.

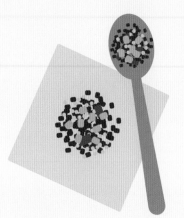

Step 2:
Hold a wonton wrapper in one hand and place a teaspoon of filling in its center.

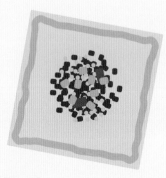

Step 3:
Dampen your finger in the water and moisten the entire edge of the wrapper.

Step 4:
Fold a corner diagonally over the filling, forming a triangle. Press the edges together to encase the filling.

Step 5:
Bring the two bottom corners together and press to seal.

HOW TO FOLD CHA GIO (SPRING ROLLS)

Step 1:
Lay out your filling, spring roll wrappers, and a plate on a work surface. In a small bowl, mix ½ cup (120 ml) water with 2 tablespoons all-purpose flour.

Step 2:
Place a wrapper on the plate with one corner pointing towards you. Fold the bottom corner up by ⅓.

Step 3:
Place about 3 tablespoons of filling along the bottom edge.

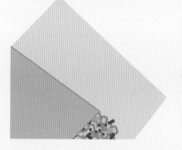

Step 4:
Fold the left corner towards the right, covering ⅔ of the filling. Fold the right corner to the left, covering the remaining filling. Wet the wrapper's edges from left to right using a dampened finger.

Step 5:
Roll the spring roll from the bottom up towards the top corner, ensuring it's tightly wrapped to minimize the risk of filling leaking during frying.

Wontons in Crispy Chili Oil

There's nothing quite like silky, well-filled wontons. The word wonton means "swallowing clouds" in Cantonese, and instantly one can imagine their delightful taste. Dip them in a savory sauce, and I promise, you won't just be swallowing clouds—you'll be floating among them. When cooking wontons, it's essential they have enough room to move around in the pot. It's better to cook them in batches than to boil everything at once.

INGREDIENTS

Wontons:
 5 ounces (150 g) raw shrimp or prawns, peeled and deveined
4 tablespoons cornstarch, divided
1 ½ teaspoons freshly ground white pepper, divided
1 teaspoon salt
1 teaspoon granulated sugar
1 tablespoon oyster sauce
1 tablespoon sesame oil
10 ounces (300 g) ground pork
¾ cup plus 2 tablespoons (200 ml) finely chopped green onions
1 ⅔ cups (400 ml) bean sprouts
1 (7-ounce/200 g) package wonton wrappers

Sauce:
3 tablespoons Crispy Chili Oil (see page 29)
2 tablespoons Crispy Shallot Oil (see page 28)
2 tablespoons light soy sauce
2 teaspoons toasted sesame oil
1 tablespoon Chinkiang vinegar (black rice vinegar)

Toppings:
⅓ cup plus 1 tablespoon (100 ml) finely chopped green onions
⅓ cup plus 1 tablespoon (100 ml) finely chopped cilantro

INSTRUCTIONS

1. Rinse the shrimp thoroughly with water and pat dry. Cut the shrimp into small pieces, roughly ¼ inch (½ cm). Place in a bowl and mix with 1 tablespoon cornstarch and ½ teaspoon pepper.

2. In a large bowl, combine the remaining 3 tablespoons cornstarch, and 1 teaspoon pepper, the salt, sugar, oyster sauce, sesame oil, and 2 tablespoons water. Add the ground pork, shrimp, and green onions, and mix well. Cover the bowl with plastic wrap and place in the refrigerator for 30 minutes.

3. While the pork-shrimp filling chills, bring a medium pot of water to a boil, add the bean sprouts, and boil for 1 minute. Drain and set aside.

4. Remove the filling from the refrigerator. Fill a small bowl with water and lay out the filling and wonton wrappers on a work surface. Place a wrapper in your hand and put a teaspoon of filling in the center. Dip a finger in the water and moisten the edge all around the wrapper. Fold one corner diagonally to the opposite corner and press the edges to seal the filling inside. Bring the two bottom corners towards the top of the dumpling. (See illustrations on page 68) Fold 10–12 wontons per person.

5. Make the sauce: in a small bowl, combine the chili oil, shallot oil, soy sauce, sesame oil, and Chinkiang.

6. Bring a large pot of water to a boil. Add the dumplings to the boiling water in batches; when they float to the surface, they are done (approximately 4–5 minutes). Remove them from the pot with a slotted spoon and transfer to a colander. Repeat until all wontons are cooked.

7. Place the dumplings in a large bowl, add the sauce and bean sprouts, and gently stir. Divide everything between 4 bowls or deep plates, and top with green onions and cilantro.

Vietnamese Bun Cha Gio with Lemongrass Pork

My family often prepares this classic Vietnamese dish during the summer, evoking the feeling of a celebration. Its numerous components—cool noodles, grilled meat, fresh herbs, and crispy spring rolls, combined with a tangy dressing—are reminiscent of a festive feast. It's ideal if the pork marinates overnight, so plan ahead.

INGREDIENTS:

1 pound (500 g) pork belly
7 ounces (200 g) thin rice noodles
Canola oil, for frying
8 fried Cha Gio (see page 75)
½ cucumber, finely julienned
6 iceberg lettuce leaves, shredded
1/3 cup plus 1 tablespoon (100 ml)
  finely chopped cilantro
1/3 cup plus 1 tablespoon (100 ml)
  Thai basil leaves
Crispy Shallot Oil, for garnish
  (see page 28)
Roasted peanuts, coarsely chopped,
  for garnish

Marinade:
½ teaspoon granulated sugar
1 tablespoon grated ginger
2 garlic cloves, minced
2 lemongrass stalks, finely chopped
2 tablespoons fish sauce
2 tablespoons light soy sauce
2 tablespoons canola oil
½ teaspoon freshly ground black
  pepper

Dressing:
3 tablespoons fish sauce
3 tablespoons granulated sugar
Juice of 4 limes
1 teaspoon finely chopped chili pepper
  (seeds removed)
1 garlic clove, grated

INSTRUCTIONS:

1. Trim the skin off the pork belly and slice it into thin strips. Place in a bowl.

2. Make the marinade: in a medium bowl, combine the sugar, ginger, garlic, lemongrass, fish sauce, soy sauce, canola oil, and pepper. Pour the marinade over the pork, stir to coat, and then cover with plastic wrap. Place the meat in the refrigerator for at least 1 ½ hours and up to overnight.

3. Make the dressing: in a medium bowl, combine the fish sauce, sugar, lime juice, chili pepper, and garlic. Add 1 ¼ cups (300 ml) water and stir until the sugar dissolves. Taste and, if necessary, add more fish sauce for saltiness, lime for acidity, or sugar for sweetness. Cover and refrigerate.

4. Place the noodles in a large bowl. Boil a generous amount of water and pour it over the noodles (there should be enough water to cover the noodles), then cover the bowl. Let the noodles sit for 10–15 minutes, occasionally lifting the lid to gently separate the noodles if they are sticking together. Taste a noodle or two as they begin to soften: you'll know they are done when they're flexible enough to wind around your finger and they have a pleasant al dente bite. Drain the noodles and rinse with cold water.

5. In a large skillet over high heat, warm a little canola oil and fry the pork belly, turning to cook on all sides, until cooked through (about 5 minutes).

6. Cut each cha gio in half crosswise. Divide the noodles between 4 deep plates, and top each with pork, cha gio, and cucumber, lettuce, cilantro, Thai basil, shallot oil, and peanuts. Drizzle each plate with the dressing.

Cha Gio (Spring Rolls)

I love fried food; there's something special about the crispiness and the flavors that arise when frying. Cha gio are spring rolls from Vietnam, and just like many Vietnamese dishes, numerous variations exist.

This recipe is my mom's version: she uses ground pork, shrimp, wood ear mushrooms, glass noodles, and turnip for the filling. The spring roll wrappers are made from wheat flour instead of the traditional rice flour. Spring rolls made with rice tend to become chewy after a while, whereas those made with wheat flour retain their crispiness longer. They're perfect to include in bun cha gio, but also great as snacks or a side dish.

INGREDIENTS:

¼ cup (30 g) plus 1 tablespoon dried wood ear mushrooms
2 ½ ounces (75 g) thin glass noodles
8 raw shrimp or prawns, peeled and deveined
10 ½ ounces (300 g) ground pork
1 yellow onion, finely chopped
¾ cup (115 g) peeled and finely chopped turnip
1 egg yolk
½ tablespoon salt
½ tablespoon freshly ground black pepper
½ tablespoon granulated sugar
½ teaspoon toasted sesame oil
1 tablespoon fish sauce
Canola oil, for frying
2 tablespoons all-purpose flour
20 spring roll wrappers (made from wheat flour)

INSTRUCTIONS

1. Soak the wood ear mushrooms in lukewarm water for 30 minutes. Drain and chop finely.

2. Place the noodles in a large bowl. Boil a generous amount of water and pour it over the noodles (there should be enough water to cover the noodles), then cover the bowl. Let the noodles sit for 10–15 minutes, occasionally lifting the lid to gently separate the noodles if they are sticking together. Taste a noodle or two as they begin to soften: you'll know they are done when they're flexible enough to wind around your finger and they have a pleasant al dente bite. Drain the noodles and rinse with cold water.

3. Thoroughly rinse the shrimp in plenty of water. Pat dry and coarsely chop.

4. In a large bowl, combine the mushrooms, noodles, shrimp, pork, onion, and turnip.

5. Add the egg yolk, salt, pepper, sugar, sesame oil, and fish sauce to the bowl. Mix well using a large spoon or your hands.

6. In a small skillet over medium-high heat, warm a bit of canola oil and fry a tablespoon of the filling. When cooked through, taste, and add more fish sauce if the filling needs more flavor and saltiness.

7. In a small bowl, combine ½ cup (120 ml) water and 2 tablespoons flour. Lay a spring roll wrapper on a plate with a corner pointing toward you. Fold up the bottom corner ⅓ of the way up the wrapper and place 3 tablespoons of filling along the bottom edge. Adjust to ensure the filling is evenly distributed.

8. Tightly fold the left and right corners over the filling, so it looks like an open envelope. Dip a finger in the water and moisten the wrapper's edges from left to right. Roll the spring roll from the bottom up towards the top corner, pulling tight to ensure the roll is firm. Continue filling and rolling until you run out of wrappers or filling. (See illustrations on page 69).

9. In a large pot over medium-high heat, heat the canola oil to 285°F (140°C). The oil should fill the pot to a depth of 2 inches (5 cm). If you don't have a thermometer, you can test the oil by dipping a dry wooden chopstick into it: if the oil bubbles around the chopstick, it's hot enough.

10. Fry the spring rolls in batches, several at a time, for approximately 10 minutes per batch or until they are crispy and golden brown. Ensure the oil does not become too hot so the outsides burn before the filling cooks through. When each batch is cooked, transfer the rolls to a plate lined with paper towels, or let them drain on a cooling rack. Repeat until all rolls are cooked.

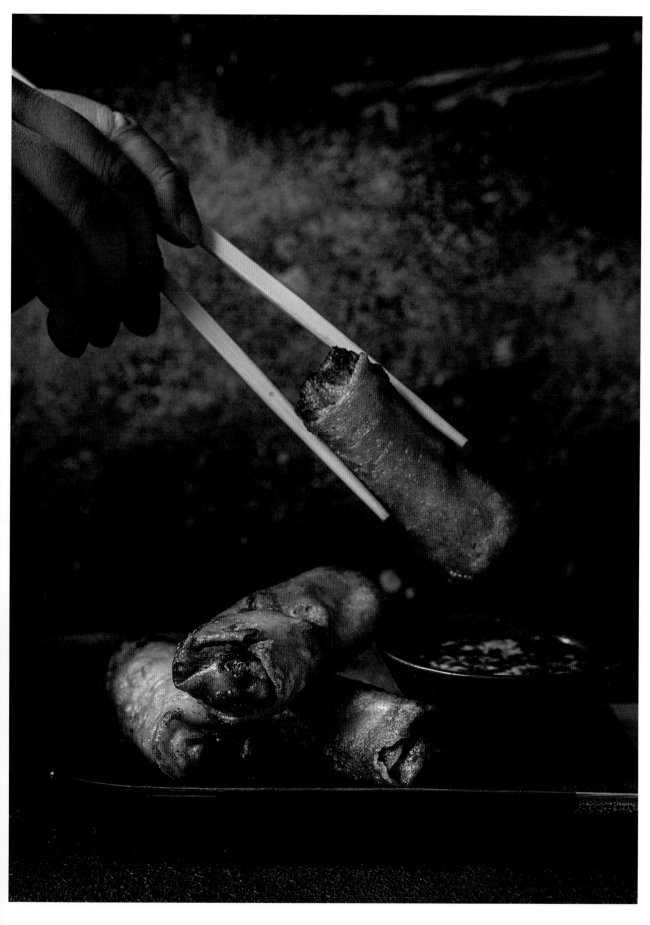

Crispy Karaage Udon with Roasted Tomatoes

Those who know me know I have a deep love for fried chicken. A cookbook without it would be incomplete. I was inspired to create this noodle dish after a dining experience in Stockholm that was so delectable it moved me to tears. This is my interpretation, enhanced with a topping of umami-rich roasted cherry tomatoes and crispy karaage (Japanese fried chicken). I often prepare a larger batch of the roasted tomatoes and save the leftovers for other dishes.

INGREDIENTS:

Roasted Tomatoes:
20 cherry tomatoes
2 tablespoons olive oil
½ teaspoon salt
½ teaspoon freshly ground
  black pepper

Karaage:
7 ounces (200 g) boneless
  skinless chicken thighs
2 tablespoons light soy sauce
1 tablespoon saké
½ tablespoon ginger juice
½ teaspoon granulated sugar
½ cup (80 g) cornstarch
Canola oil, for frying

4 ounces (180 g) udon noodles
2 tablespoons unsalted butter
1 garlic clove, finely chopped
1 teaspoon finely chopped
  ginger
½ cup (52 g) finely chopped
  green onions, divided
1 tablespoon gochujang
1 tablespoon Crispy Chili Oil
  (see page 29)
2 tablespoons Kewpie
  mayonnaise, divided
1 tablespoon yuzu juice, divided
Roasted sesame seeds,
  for garnish

INSTRUCTIONS:

1. Make the roasted tomatoes: preheat the oven to 230°F (110°C). Halve the tomatoes and place them in a bowl. Drizzle with the olive oil, season with the salt and pepper, then lay them cut side up on a baking sheet lined with parchment paper. Bake in the center of the oven for 3 hours.

2. Make the karaage: when the tomatoes have 40 minutes left to roast, cut the chicken into 2-inch pieces. In a large bowl, combine the soy sauce, saké, ginger juice, and sugar. Add the chicken, turning to coat, and let marinate for 10 minutes at room temperature.

3. Place the cornstarch in a large bowl. Coat each chicken piece fully in the cornstarch and set aside on a plate. Once all pieces are coated, let them rest for 5 minutes. This allows the cornstarch to adhere and form a layer that becomes crispy upon frying.

4. In a large pot over medium-high heat, heat the canola oil to about 360°F (180°C). The oil should fill the pot to a depth of 2 inches (5 cm). If you don't have a thermometer, you can test the oil by dipping a dry wooden chopstick into it: if the oil bubbles around the chopstick, it's hot enough.

5. Fry the chicken in batches to maintain the oil's temperature. Triple fry for ultimate crispiness: 5 minutes initially, then 2 minutes for the subsequent two sessions. In between frying, drain the fried chicken on paper towels. Repeat until all chicken is fried.

6. Cook the udon noodles as per the package instructions or until al dente. Rinse with cold water.

7. In a large skillet over medium-high heat, melt the butter. Add the garlic, ginger, and half of the green onions and sauté for 1 minute. Add gochujang and chili oil and cook for an additional 2 minutes.

8. Add the noodles to the skillet mixture and stir until well-coated. Divide between 2 bowls. To each bowl, add 1 tablespoon of mayonnaise and ½ tablespoon of yuzu juice, and stir to mix. Top each bowl with roasted tomatoes, karaage, sesame seeds, and the remaining green onions.

Dan Dan Noodles

Dan dan noodles are an incredibly popular Sichuan street food dish: springy noodles served in a spicy sauce with rich flavors, crispy minced meat, coarsely chopped nuts, and bok choy. Different restaurants in China have their unique versions of the dish, and this is how I make mine.

INGREDIENTS:

1 head bok choy
4 ounces (125 g) servings wheat
 noodles
1 tablespoon canola oil
3 ounces (100 g) ground pork
 (or other ground beef or
 plant-based meat)
1 tablespoon black bean sauce
 or hoisin sauce
1 teaspoon dark soy sauce
Freshly ground black pepper
¼ cup (26 g) finely chopped green
 onions, for garnish
¼ cup (33 g) coarsely chopped
 roasted and salted peanuts,
 for garnish

Sauce:
2 tablespoons sesame paste
1 tablespoon peanut butter
1 garlic clove, grated
2 tablespoons light soy sauce
1 tablespoon Chinkiang vinegar
 (black rice vinegar)
1 teaspoon granulated sugar
Freshly ground Sichuan pepper
2 tablespoons Crispy Chili Oil,
 plus more for garnish
 (see page 29)

INSTRUCTIONS:

1. Bring a pot of water to a boil. Separate the bok choy into leaves and add them to the pot; boil for 1 minute. Drain and set aside.

2. Cook the noodles as per package instructions or until al dente. Before draining, reserve about ½ cup (120 ml) of the noodle water. Drain the noodles and rinse them in cold water.

3. Make the sauce: in a medium bowl, mix the sesame paste and peanut butter with the reserved warm noodle water. Add the garlic, soy sauce, Chinkiang, sugar, Sichuan pepper to taste, and the chili oil. Stir until the sugar dissolves.

4. In a medium skillet over medium-high heat, warm the canola oil. Add the ground pork and let it sear on one side. After 2 minutes, stir and continue to fry until meat is slightly crispy. Stir in the bean or hoisin sauce and cook for 1 minute. Add the soy sauce, ¼ cup (60 ml) water, and black pepper to taste. Reduce the heat and simmer for 2 minutes.

5. Divide the noodles and sauce between 2 bowls. Top with the cooked meat, bok choy leaves, green onions, peanuts, and more chili oil and Sichuan pepper if desired for added heat.

Slurpy Noodles with Fried Chili Corn

This noodle dish is drenched in an aromatic sauce, boasting flavors from doubanjiang, Sichuan pepper, and fish sauce, and then topped with green onions and crispy, golden fried corn. Don't forget napkins; it's delightfully messy!

INGREDIENTS:

6 shallots, thinly sliced
Generous ¾ cup (200 ml) canola oil
8 green onions, coarsely chopped, divided
3 tablespoons doubanjiang (fermented fava beans)
½ cup (120 ml) light soy sauce
1 tablespoon Chinkiang vinegar (black rice vinegar)
2 tablespoons fish sauce
1 ½ tablespoons granulated sugar
2 tablespoons freshly ground Sichuan pepper
½ teaspoon freshly ground white pepper
8 ounces (250 g) kuan miao noodles

Fried Chili Corn:
14 ounces (400 g) corn kernels, from about 4 ears of corn
3 tablespoons cornstarch
2 ⅓ cups (550 ml) cold carbonated water (or beer)
2 cups (120 g) all-purpose flour
3 tablespoons Crispy Chili Oil (see page 29)
2 large eggs
½ teaspoon baking powder
Canola oil, for frying

INSTRUCTIONS:

1. Place the shallots in a saucepan and pour the canola oil over them; it should completely cover them. Turn the heat to medium and fry the shallots until golden. Be mindful, as the shallots can burn easily. Turn off the heat and let the shallots cool.

2. In another saucepan over medium-high heat, warm 2 tablespoons of the Crispy Chili Oil. . Add half the green onions and sauté until edges are slightly browned.

3. To the same saucepan as the green onions, add the doubanjiang and sauté for 2 minutes. Transfer the mixture to a blender along with soy sauce, Chinkiang, fish sauce, sugar, Sichuan pepper, and white pepper. Add the shallots. Drizzle with the remaining Crispy Chili Oil and then blend until smooth. Set the sauce aside.

4. Make the fried chili corn: in a medium bowl, combine the corn kernels, cornstarch, carbonated water or beer, flour, eggs, and baking powder. Stir well to combine.

5. In a large pot over medium-high heat, heat a generous inch of the canola oil to about 340°F (170°C). If you don't have a thermometer, you can test the oil by dipping a dry wooden chopstick into it: if the oil bubbles around the chopstick, it's hot enough.

6. Using a spoon, drop dollops of corn mixture into the hot oil and fry until golden. Drain the fried corn on paper towels.

7. Cook noodles as per package instructions or until al dente. Drain and divide between 4 bowls. Add sauce to each bowl and stir to coat the noodles.

8. Top with the remaining chopped green onions and the fried corn.

9. Store any leftover sauce in a tightly sealed glass jar and refrigerate for up to 2 months.

Cantonese Crispy Shrimp

The combination of roasted salt and pepper can be found in many Cantonese dishes, crispy shrimp being one of them. My mother ensures this dish is present at every festive meal. Many Chinese people are superstitious, and my mother is no exception. Eating foods whose names sound like other auspicious words is customary during festivities. In Cantonese, the word for "shrimp" sounds like the word for "laughter," so consuming lots of shrimp ensures a life filled with laughter. Delicious shrimp and endless joy? I'm in!

INGREDIENTS:

Sauce:
1 tablespoon oyster sauce
1 tablespoon light soy sauce
1 tablespoon toasted sesame oil
1 tablespoon granulated sugar

1 teaspoon salt
1 teaspoon coarsely ground
   black pepper
12 raw shrimp (or prawns),
   shells on
2 tablespoons cornstarch
3 ⅓ cups (800 ml) canola oil,
   for frying, plus 2 tablespoons
   canola oil
2 shallots, chopped
½ yellow onion, finely chopped
3 large medium-hot red chili
   peppers, chopped
6 garlic cloves, chopped
8 ounces (250 g) egg noodles
1 cup (100 g) chopped green
   onions

INSTRUCTIONS:

1. Make the sauce: in a bowl, combine the oyster sauce, soy sauce, sesame oil, sugar, and ½ cup (120 ml) water. Stir until the sugar dissolves. Set aside.

2. Place a small skillet over medium-high heat. Add the salt and toast for 2 minutes, stirring occasionally. Turn off the heat, add the pepper, and roast for another minute, making sure the pepper doesn't burn. Transfer the salt and pepper to a bowl and let cool.

3. Sprinkle the shrimp with salt on both sides, then let sit for 5 minutes. Rinse the shrimp with water and then pat dry. Trim the shrimp by snipping off the legs but retaining the shell. Cut open the back of each shrimp to remove any veins. In a medium bowl, combine the shrimp and cornstarch and toss to coat.

4. In a large pot over medium-high heat, heat 3 1/3 cups of the canola oil to 350°F (175°C), making sure the oil is at least 1 ½ inches (4 cm) from the top of the pot. If you don't have a thermometer, you can test the oil by dipping a dry wooden chopstick into it: if the oil bubbles around the chopstick, it's hot enough.

5. Fry the shrimp carefully, a few at a time, for about 3 minutes, or until golden and crispy. Transfer carefully to paper towels to drain.

6. In a large skillet over medium-high heat, warm the remaining 2 tablespoons of canola oil. Add the shallots and onion and sauté for 2 minutes. Add the chili peppers and garlic, and sauté for 1 more minute. Transfer half the onion-chili pepper mix to a bowl and leave the rest in the skillet.

7. Pour the sauce into the skillet and simmer over medium-low heat until the sauce is slightly reduced. Add the shrimp to the skillet and stir to coat with the sauce.

8. Cook the noodles as per package instructions or until al dente. Drain and divide between 4 bowls. Top each bowl with shrimp and sauce.

9. Top each bowl with green onions, a sprinkle of roasted salt and pepper, and the reserved onion-chili pepper mix.

A Memory of Food

The China Bus

Growing up, a ritual occurred every Friday at 3 p.m. My entire family would gather in the parking lot next to the pizzeria to await the arrival of the China Bus. The China Bus was a mobile Asian grocery store, stocked with everything you could imagine. This unique vehicle had its typical seats removed, making room for shelves and crates filled with Asian products and ingredients. As a child, my attention was captivated by the array of snacks and candies that I might persuade my parents to buy me, if I was lucky. My absolute favorite were the small jellies in various fruit flavors, with lychee being the most delightful.

I can only imagine the gratitude my parents felt toward the individual who operated this bus, allowing them access to Asian products that would have otherwise been nearly impossible to acquire. Nowadays, when I wander through Asian grocery stores, I often find myself reflecting nostalgically on that bus, recalling the murmurs of eager customers and familiar scents.
I'm profoundly grateful for a childhood where our culinary heritage was celebrated.

RAMEN

The small noodle packets commonly referred to as instant noodles are actually a budget version of the Japanese noodle dish known as ramen. In Japan, these are termed "instant ramen." Originating from the Chinese noodle dish lamian, ramen is a relatively young dish, with just over a century of history. Throughout its existence, countless variations have emerged, and it continues to be a dish subject to much experimentation.

A bowl of ramen is typically made up of five components: broth, noodles, tare, oil, and toppings. Each of these elements can vary in many ways, which explains why ramen restaurants the world around offer dishes with such distinct flair and unique character—a fact that exhilarates me each time I visit a new ramen establishment. In this chapter, I will provide insights into how each of the five components of ramen can be constructed, and share some of my favorite recipes.

RAMEN'S FIVE COMPONENTS

〜

It's often said that a perfect bowl of ramen comprises five foundational components: broth, noodles, tare, aromatic oil, and toppings.

Broth

The broth sets the stage for an exceptional ramen. Usually, the first taste of the dish is drawn from the broth. The base for a broth is typically chicken, pork, seafood, and/or vegetables, and the secret to a compelling broth is extracting as much flavor and richness from the ingredients as possible. The depth of the broth, also called "body," usually originates from fats and bones.

Noodles

Ramen noodles are traditionally crafted from wheat flour, water, salt, and kansui (an alkaline ingredient that is necessary to make ramen). The interaction between water and flour, formed by the bonds between starch and gluten, results in the noodles' structure, while the kansui reacts with the protein in flour, endowing the noodles with their distinctive elasticity and chewy texture, a characteristic unique to ramen noodles. Salt primarily strengthens the structure of the noodles, and adds flavor.

Tare

This component operates discreetly behind the scenes in a ramen dish but nevertheless amplifies the broth. Tare serves as a pivotal flavor enhancer for the broth, introducing umami, salinity, and a delightful depth. It remains the secret weapon of many chefs, its specific ingredients often guarded closely. Some common tare ingredients include soy sauce, saké, seaweed, dried fish, miso, and salt. Tares are often named based on their primary flavor; for instance, a salt-based tare is called shio tare (*shio* means "salt") while a soy-based one is termed shoyu tare (*shoyu* means "soy").

Aromatic Oil

The oil added to ramen is a component that often goes unnoticed. It's usually flavored with various aromatic ingredients and floats to the surface of the bowl. The nature of oil helps retain extracted flavors that might otherwise dilute in water. When the noodles are immersed in the broth, they acquire a coating from this oil, giving them a smooth surface. The oil also acts as a thermal barrier, preventing the broth's temperature from dropping too quickly.

Toppings

There is a vast array of ramen toppings from which to choose, and toppings are the components that are most experimented with. Besides tasting divine, toppings ideally also should be visually appealing. The most classic toppings include menma (fermented bamboo shoots), chashu (pork belly), green onions, seaweed, and ajitsuke tamago (soft-boiled eggs).

My preferred method of assembling ramen is as follows:

1. POUR TARE AND OIL INTO THE BOWL.

2. ADD WARM BROTH.

3. INTRODUCE COOKED NOODLES.

4. PLACE TOPPINGS ON TOP.

MAKING YOUR OWN NOODLES

One of my cherished memories from childhood is watching my mother make noodles at our kitchen table. I'd sit next to her, observing how meticulously and accurately she weighed each ingredient. Her hands mixed the ingredients in a practiced, deliberate manner. Flour would spread across the table, and she'd roll out the dough, working it through the pasta machine as if she'd done it a million times before.

I always insisted on helping by turning the crank while she fed the dough and caught it on the other side. Out would come perfect noodles, carefully shaped into portion-sized bundles. The chicken broth, simmering since morning, awaited the freshly made noodles. She'd swiftly cook the noodles in a pot of boiling water, strain them, and then serve them up in a bowl with steaming broth and a medley of toppings.

Eating her artisanal noodles, paired with the broth and accompaniments, was immensely satisfying—they were truly a favorite of mine. It's a craft I now work at diligently, hoping to master it someday. While there's still a journey ahead, it's just like any practice: sometimes I succeed, and sometimes I don't quite hit the mark. I always expect an occasional noodle that's not quite up to par.

The tricky part of noodle-making lies in getting the precise amounts of each ingredient just right. The ratios can greatly influence the final texture and taste. Other factors, seemingly mundane, are in fact critical—like the protein content in the flour, water hardness, room humidity, or even the type of salt used. For this reason, many ramen restaurants in Japan often resort to using premade noodles for their dishes.

So, why embark on this culinary endeavor, striving to perfect something so intricate? For me, it's about preserving an age-old craft. Making my own noodles is my way of narrating a tale passed down through generations, a legacy I hope continues. After all, isn't the feeling of accomplishing a challenging feat rewarding?

Toasted Ramen Noodles

Why bother making your own noodles when you can buy them ready-made? Honestly, while I love the abundance of excellent and delicious store-bought options, homemade noodles are in a league of their own. The satisfaction derived from savoring one's own creation is unparalleled.

The best part? It doesn't require much manual kneading. Leave the labor to the pasta machine, which produces slurp-worthy noodles. In this recipe, I've opted for various flours to lend unique dimensions in flavor and texture, something I feel is missed when using just one type. It's imperative to use a scale for accurate measurements so I have included even the teaspoon weights in the recipe. 00 flour is a finely ground flour from Italy, but you can substitute all-purpose flour if you can't find 00.

INGREDIENTS:

1 ¼ teaspoons (6 grams)
  Kansui (see page 96)
1 ¼ teaspoons (6 grams) salt
⅓ cup (40 grams) coarse rye
  flour
3 ⅔ cups (460 grams) 00 flour
Cornstarch, for dusting

Special equipment: a pasta
  machine

INSTRUCTIONS:

1. In a medium bowl, combine the kansui and salt. Add ¾ cup (180 grams) of cold water and stir to dissolve the kansui and salt.

2. In a dry skillet over medium heat, add the rye flour and toast, stirring continuously to ensure it doesn't burn. The flour shouldn't change color. Remove from heat once a roasted aroma emerges. Sift the flour through a sifter or fine-mesh sieve, then transfer to a large bowl.

3. Add the 00 flour to the bowl and mix to combine with the rye flour. Slowly pour in the kansui water mixture, and with your hands, knead the mixture into a rough ball. The dough will be somewhat dry and crumbly—this is expected. Wrap the dough in plastic wrap and let it rest at room temperature for 1 hour.

4. After an hour, the dough will still be a bit dry, but should be easier to work with. Use a knife to divide the dough into four equal parts. Wrap the pieces you're not working with in plastic wrap so they don't dry out.

5. Set the pasta machine to its widest setting. Press the dough into a rectangle using your hands. Process it through the pasta machine—it may initially fall apart and be challenging to piece together. Continue shaping it into a rectangle and run it through the machine several times. Once the dough starts holding together, fold it once and repeat the process until smooth, roughly 20 folds.

6. Adjust the setting to one notch thinner and process through the machine in the same manner—fold, run through—twice. Continue in this fashion, adjusting the setting until you find a thickness you're satisfied with. I usually prefer my noodles at thickness level 4. If the noodle sheet becomes too long, feel free to cut it in half or to your desired length.

7. Attach the cutting roller and pass the sheet through to shape the noodles. As they emerge, dust them lightly with cornstarch and coil the noodles into a nest. Repeat with the remaining three dough portions.

8. Arrange the noodles in portions on a plate, wrap with plastic wrap, and refrigerate. They last for 2 days. Or, to freeze the noodles, place them in portions on a tray and put in the freezer. Once they are frozen, transfer the portions into freezer bags. They will keep for 3 months.

To cook: I cook homemade ramen noodles the same way as regular wheat noodles—in a large pot with plenty of boiling water and 1 teaspoon salt per quart. The cooking time for homemade ramen noodles varies depending on their thickness. Thin noodles cook faster, while thicker ones need a little more time. Noodles I make at thickness level 4 require about 30 seconds to cook. The best way to determine the perfect cooking time for your noodles is to test a few. When the noodles are cooked, drain them thoroughly to remove as much starch as possible. If you're using the noodles for cold dishes that won't be added to soup, rinse them with plenty of cold water to halt the cooking and remove all the starch.

Kansui

MAKES 1/4 CUP (56 G) 〜〜 **1 HOUR**

Adding an alkaline substance to wheat dough changes its pH value. This fosters more connections between the gluten strands, leading to a denser and firmer dough. With a firmer dough, the noodles have a chewy texture, are more resilient, and absorb less liquid, which is desirable when noodles are immersed in warm broth.

INGREDIENTS:

¼ cup (56 g) baking soda

INSTRUCTIONS:

1. Preheat the oven to 250°F (120°C).

2. Line a baking sheet with aluminum foil. Spread the baking soda in an even layer.

3. Transfer the sheet to the center rack of the oven and roast for 1 hour.

4. Remove the sheet from the oven, let the baking powder cool, and then transfer to a clean glass jar. Seal the jar tightly, and ensure it remains closed most of the time, as the powder can easily absorb moisture and lose its effectiveness. Store in a dark, cool place for up to 2 months.

Chashu

When it comes to toppings for steaming ramen, chashu (Japanese pork belly) is one of my favorites. Whenever I have ramen at a restaurant, I usually order extra. A perfect piece of chashu, in my opinion, should have an even mix of fat and meat, and be cooked slowly. It's best to prepare the meat a day in advance as it's easier to slice when cooled (cutting the meat immediately might cause it to fall apart). Chashu is excellent as a topping for ramen, but it's also a great side for various dishes, such as stir-fries.

INGREDIENTS:

2 pounds (1 kg) pork belly,
  skin removed
5 cilantro sprigs (or 1 tablespoon
  coriander seeds), washed
3 green onions, trimmed and cut
  into 3 segments each
1 ½-inch piece ginger, peeled
  and quartered
4 garlic cloves, skins on, crushed
1 yellow onion, quartered
1 star anise pod
2 tablespoons brown sugar
  or granulated sugar
½ tablespoon black peppercorns
¼ cup (60 ml) mirin
½ cup (120 ml) light soy sauce
¼ cup (60 ml) dark soy sauce
¼ cup (60 ml) saké or dry sherry

INSTRUCTIONS:

1. Cut the pork belly into three equal pieces. Alternatively, you can roll up the entire piece and tie it with string. Place the pieces in a large pot.

2. Add the cilantro, green onions, ginger, garlic, onion, star anise, sugar, peppercorns, mirin, soy sauce, and saké. Fill the pot with water until the meat is just covered.

3. Cover the pot and bring to a boil. Reduce the heat to low until the liquid is at a gentle simmer. Keep the pot covered, but check and turn the meat every hour. Cook for up to 4 hours, adding water if necessary to keep the meat covered, until it is tender.

4. Remove the pot from the heat. Carefully lift the meat from the pot, place it on a plate, and let it cool. Wrap the meat in plastic wrap and store it in the refrigerator.

5. Strain the liquid into another pot and set over medium heat. Reduce the liquid until its consistency begins to resemble a sauce. Remove from heat and let cool. Pour into a lidded clean jar and store in the refrigerator for up to one week. (Beyond ramen, this sauce is delicious in various stir-fries with noodles, rice, or vegetables, and also serves as a great flavor enhancer, especially for instant noodles.)

6. To serve the chashu with ramen, slice the meat to your desired thickness and pan-fry, sear with a torch, warm in an oven at 210°F (100°C), or heat it in the soup when serving.

Ajitsuke Tamago

Salty, sweet, and creamy with a profound umami flavor—that's the best way to describe these marinated soft-boiled eggs. Not only are they a favorite topping for ramen, but they also make perfect snacks or accompaniments to other Southeast Asian rice dishes.

INGREDIENTS:

6 large eggs
⅔ cup (160 ml) light soy sauce
¼ cup (60 ml) mirin
¼ cup (60 ml) saké
1 ½-inch piece ginger, peeled and coarsely diced

INSTRUCTIONS:

1. Fill a medium pot with water and bring to a boil. Gently place the eggs into boiling water, reduce the heat to medium, and cook for 6 minutes and 30 seconds. While eggs boil, prepare a bowl of ice water. Use a slotted spoon to transfer the eggs to the ice water. Let cool for 5 minutes.

2. While eggs cook, in a small saucepan, combine 1 ¼ cups (300 ml) water and the soy sauce, mirin, saké, and ginger. Heat the mixture over medium heat until it just begins to boil, then remove from the stove, pour into a jar with a lid (large enough to hold the eggs), and let cool.

3. Carefully peel the eggs and add them to the liquid. Be sure they are fully submerged. Seal with the lid.

4. Refrigerate and allow the eggs to marinate, preferably for at least 24 hours, before consuming. They'll keep for about 3 days. Note: The yolk's consistency changes from the first to the third day, becoming firmer and saltier the longer it sits in the liquid.

Menma

Meaning "flavored bamboo," menma is a classic ramen topping but can also be enjoyed just as a snack. With a little care and attention, ordinary bamboo shoots transform into a delectable treat.

INGREDIENTS:

1 (8-ounce/250-g) can preserved bamboo shoots, whole or sliced
½ chicken or vegetable bouillon cube
2 tablespoons sesame oil
1 tablespoon saké
1 tablespoon light soy sauce
2 teaspoons mirin

INSTRUCTIONS:

1. Drain the bamboo shoots and rinse them thoroughly with water. If you bought whole shoots, cut them into slices about 1/8 inch (⅓ cm) thick and 1 ½–2 inches (3 ¾–5 cm) long.

2. In a small saucepan or electric kettle, bring a few cups of water to a boil. Place the bamboo shoots in a strainer, and pour the boiling water over them (to wash away any lingering canned scent).

3. Warm ½ cup (120 ml) water in a pot on the stove or in a container in the microwave. Add the bouillon cube and stir to dissolve.

4. In a medium skillet over medium heat, warm the sesame oil in a frying pan and sauté the bamboo shoots for 2–3 minutes.

5. Pour the dissolved bouillon liquid, saké, soy sauce, and mirin into the frying pan, and cook, stirring, until the liquid is almost entirely reduced.

6. Turn off the heat, add a few drops of sesame oil, and stir. Let the bamboo shoots cool, then store them in a clean glass jar in the refrigerator for up to 4 days.

Shio Tare

MAKES: ABOUT 2 CUPS (120 G) ∿ **10 MINUTES (+ SOAKING FOR 3 HOURS)**

"Shio" translates to "salt" in Japanese. Shio tare is one of the primary flavoring agents in ramen. A good shio tare in the right quantity accentuates the various tastes in the dish it's used in, just as salt does.

INGREDIENTS

3 sheets kombu
6 dried shiitake mushrooms
2 ½ tablespoons salt

INSTRUCTIONS

1. Cut the kombu into large pieces using scissors and place it in a pot. Add the mushrooms and about 2 ½ cups (600 ml) water. Let it sit for at least 3 hours.

2. Incorporate the salt into the mixture and bring everything to a boil, stirring until the salt has dissolved. Let it cool, strain, and store in a clean glass jar in the refrigerator.

Shoyu Tare

MAKES: ABOUT 1.25 CUPS (300 ML) 〜 **15 MINUTES**

"Shoyu," the Japanese term for soy sauce, is the oldest flavoring and is widely popular in ramen. Along with its soy base, ingredients like kombu, katsuobushi, saké, and mirin are added, giving the sauce added depth and a richer umami flavor.

INGREDIENTS

6 tablespoons mirin
4 tablespoons saké
1 tablespoon granulated sugar
½ cup (120 ml) light soy sauce
1/4 cup (60 ml) dark soy sauce
2 x 2 inch (5 x 5 cm) piece of kombu
1 cup (240 ml) katsuobushi
   (bonito flakes)

INSTRUCTIONS

1. In a saucepan, combine mirin, saké, and sugar, and bring it to a boil for 2 minutes.

2. Add both the light and dark soy sauces, reduce heat, and simmer for 1 minute.

3. Add the kombu and katsuobushi and continue to simmer for roughly 10 minutes. Do not allow the liquid to boil becaue katsuobushi can turn bitter when exposed to high temperatures.

4. Remove the pan from the heat and allow the sauce cool. Strain and store in a clean jar in the refrigerator.

Sofrito

Across the world, many cuisines start dishes with a base made of different ingredients. This base goes by different names depending on the country, such as sofrito, sofregit, soffritto, or refogado, to name a few. Sofrito is an aromatic base made of ingredients that have been carefully and slowly cooked over low heat. It accentuates and works wonders in the dishes it's used in, giving the flavors added depth. It's an excellent component to incorporate into ramen. An oven-safe cast-iron pot is the best cooking vessel, but if you don't have one you can start the dish in a pot on the stove and then transfer to an oven-safe dish covered with foil.

INGREDIENTS:

2 apples, peeled and finely diced
3 yellow onions, finely chopped
Scant 2 cups (450 ml) canola oil
12 garlic cloves, finely chopped
3 x 3-inch (8 x 8-cm) piece ginger,
   peeled and finely diced

INSTRUCTIONS:

1. Preheat the oven to 230°F (110°C).

2. Place apples and onions in an oven-safe cast-iron pot. Add the oil, set the pot over low-medium heat, and warm until it starts to bubble and the ingredients begin to sweat. Put on the lid and place the pot in the oven, letting it cook for about 3 hours, lifting the lid and stirring occasionally to ensure nothing sticks to the bottom. The onions and apples should cook slowly and not take on any color until the end of the cooking time.

3. Once the onions and apples begin to brown, add the garlic and ginger to the pot. Continue cooking for another 2–3 hours, stirring occasionally. The mixture should become creamy and light brown.

4. Remove the pot from the oven, let the sofrito cool, and then transfer to an airtight container and store in the refrigerator for up to 2 weeks.

Mushroom Broth

The key to a delicious broth lies in umami and deep flavors. With animal products, achieving this is straightforward; typically, it only requires a protein, such as chicken, and water. However, coaxing umami and deep flavors from a vegan broth can be more challenging. Therefore, it's essential to use numerous umami-rich ingredients, like dried shiitake mushrooms, dried seaweed, and roasted vegetables like yellow onion. This broth is a perfect substitute for other broths called for in recipes in this book—experiment and find your favorite!

INGREDIENTS:

½ head of lettuce
2-inch (5-cm) piece ginger, peeled and sliced
4 garlic cloves, peeled and halved
1 yellow onion, peeled and halved
2 carrots, roughly chopped
6 green onions, trimmed
4- to 6-inch (10–15 cm) piece radish, roughly chopped
2 tablespoons canola oil
15 dried shiitake mushrooms
3 x 3-inch (8 x 8-cm) piece kombu
4 tablespoons vegan tsuyu
1 teaspoon MSG
Salt

INSTRUCTIONS:

1. Preheat the oven to 400°F (200°C). Rinse the lettuce and cut in half lengthwise. Place the lettuce, ginger, garlic, onion, carrots, green onions, and radish on a baking sheet, and drizzle the canola oil over it. Toss to coat the ingredients with the oil. Place in the oven and roast for 15 minutes in the oven. Then turn the oven to broil and broil for 5 minutes.

2. Fill a large pot with 1 gallon (4 liters) of water and add the roasted vegetables, mushrooms, kombu, and tsuyu. Place over medium heat and bring to a simmer. Reduce the heat to low, and position two chopsticks, one on each side at the edge of the pot, before placing the lid on the pot. (This eases the pressure and simplifies monitoring the simmering.) Maintain a gentle simmer for 3 hours.

3. Turn off the heat, strain the broth, retaining the vegetables, and season with the MSG and salt to taste. The mushrooms, radish, and carrot can be consumed with the broth or used as a topping for other dishes.

Spicy Miso Ramen

If I were to select a signature dish from this book, it would undoubtedly be this spicy miso ramen—I've prepared it countless times. This recipe requires some planning, but much can be done ahead of time. From your first sip to the last, I promise you will experience pure satisfaction. There's a reason I love making it. For this recipe (and all other ramen recipes), you should eat your ramen immediately once it's ready, as the noodles will continue cooking in the hot soup. If you let the dish sit for a while, the noodles will become overcooked and lose their delightful texture.

INGREDIENTS:

Broth:
3 ⅓ cups (800 ml) Mom's Chicken
   Broth (see page 127)

Tare:
2 tablespoons red miso
2 tablespoons white miso
1 teaspoon toasted sesame oil
1 teaspoon Chinkiang vinegar
   (black rice vinegar)
3 tablespoons Crispy Chili Oil
(see page 29)
½ teaspoon MSG

Toppings:
5 ½ ounces (150 g) Chashu
   (see page 99)
2 Ajitsuke Tamago (see page 101)
¾ cup (200 g) bean sprouts
½ cup (25 g) finely chopped cilantro
½ cup (52 g) finely chopped
green onions
Toasted sesame seeds
Dried chili pepper threads

Aromatic Oil:
2 tablespoons Sofrito
(see page 107)
2 tablespoons Crispy Shallot Oil
   (see page 28)

Noodles:
4 ounces (125 g) ramen noodles,
   homemade (see page 92)
   or store-bought

INSTRUCTIONS:

1. In a medium pot over medium heat, bring the broth to a simmer. While broth warms, make the tare: In a bowl, combine both misos, the sesame oil, Chinkiang, chili oil, and MSG. Pour about ¼ cup of the hot broth into the tare, and stir until the miso is dissolved. Add this mixture to the simmering broth. Taste and adjust with chili oil for extra heat if desired. Reduce the heat to low to keep the broth warm.

2. Prepare the toppings: slice the meat to the desired thickness and cut the eggs in half. Bring a small pot of water to a boil, add the bean sprouts, and boil for 1 minute. Drain and set aside. Set out the other toppings.

3. Set out 2 large ramen bowls, and place 1 tablespoon of sofrito and 1 tablespoon of shallot oil in each.

4. Warm the chashu either by frying it in a skillet, using a torch, or warming it in the oven at 210°F (100°C). Alternatively, allow the soup to warm the meat upon serving.

5. In a medium pot, bring a generous amount of water to a rolling boil. Add the noodles and cook until al dente. Drain thoroughly to remove as much starch as possible.

6. Divide the noodles between the 2 bowls, pour in the broth, and top with the chashu, eggs, bean sprouts, cilantro, green onions, sesame seeds, and chili pepper strands. Serve immediately.

Shoyu Ramen

This bowl of ramen is based on the flavoring of shoyu tare, a concentrated sauce made primarily from soy, seaweed, and dried tuna. The tare, chicken broth, quality noodles, and minimalistic toppings combine to create a simple yet profoundly flavorful ramen.

INGREDIENTS:

Broth:
3 ⅓ cups (800 ml) Mom's Chicken Broth (see page 127)
½ teaspoon MSG

Tare:
4 tablespoons Shoyu Tare (see page 105)

Aromatic Oil:
2 tablespoons Sofrito (see page 107)
2 tablespoons Crispy Shallot Oil (see page 28)

Noodles:
4 ounces (125 g) ramen noodles, homemade (see page 92) or store-bought

Toppings:
5 ½ ounces (150 g) Chashu (see page 99)
2 Ajitsuke Tamago (see page 101)
8 slices Menma (see page 103)
4 sheets nori
½ cup (52 g) finely chopped green onions

INSTRUCTIONS:

1. In a medium pot over medium heat, bring the broth to a simmer. Stir in the MSG. Reduce the heat to low to keep the broth warm.

2. Prepare the toppings: slice the meat to the desired thickness and cut the eggs in half. Set out the other toppings.

3. Set out 2 large ramen bowls, and add 2 tablespoons of shoyu tare, 1 tablespoon sofrito, and 1 tablespoon shallot oil to each.

4. Warm the chashu either by frying it in a skillet, using a torch, or warming it in the oven at 210°F (100°C). Alternatively, allow the soup to warm the meat upon serving.

5. In a medium pot, bring a generous amount of water to a rolling boil. Add the noodles and cook until al dente. Drain thoroughly to remove as much starch as possible.

6. Pour broth into the bowls, stirring briefly to blend with the tare, sofrito, and shallot oil. Divide the noodles between the bowls and top with the chashu, eggs, menma, nori, and green onions. Serve immediately.

Yuzu Clam Shio Ramen

Shio tare gives this ramen a salty flavor base. The foundation is a deep broth complemented by aromatic sofrito, ocean flavors from clams, creaminess from coconut, and the freshness of yuzu—put together, these ingredients create an irresistible combination.

INGREDIENTS:

Broth:
1 ¾ pounds (875 g) clams
Salt
2 tablespoons canola oil
3 garlic cloves, finely chopped
1 ¼-inch (3-cm) piece ginger, peeled and finely chopped
1 shallot, finely chopped
Generous ¾ cup (200 ml) saké or dry sherry
4 ¼ cups (1 liter) Mom's Chicken Broth (see page 127)
3 tablespoons fish sauce
2 teaspoons Chinkiang vinegar (black rice vinegar)
1 cup (240 ml) coconut milk
3 tablespoons yuzu juice

Tare:
8 tablespoons Shio Tare (see page 104)

Aromatic Oil:
8 tablespoons Sofrito (see page 107)

Noodles:
8 ounces (250 g) ramen noodles, homemade (see page 95) or store-bought

Topping:
½ cup (25 g) chopped cilantro

INSTRUCTIONS:

1. Rinse the clams, discarding any with broken shells or shells that don't close. Fill a large bowl with water and add 2 tablespoons salt. Add the clams and let soak for 30 minutes. Drain and rinse.

2. In a large pot or Dutch oven over medium heat, warm the oil and add the garlic, ginger, and shallot. Sauté for 2 minutes. Raise the heat to medium-high, and add the clams and saké. Cover the pot and cook for 10 minutes, until the clams open and cook through.

3. Reduce the heat to medium, remove the clams with a slotted spoon, and set aside.

4. Add the chicken broth, fish sauce, Chinkiang, and coconut milk to the pot. Bring to a simmer, and add the yuzu juice and more salt to taste.

5. Set out 2 large ramen bowls, and add 2 tablespoons shio tare and 2 tablespoons sofrito to each.

6. In a large pot, bring a generous amount of water to a rolling boil. Add the noodles and cook until al dente. Drain thoroughly to remove as much starch as possible.

7. Divide the noodles between the bowls, pour over the broth, and top with clams and cilantro. Serve immediately.

Birria Taco Ramen

Have you ever heard of birria taco ramen? Let me explain. I've always believed certain elements of Mexican and Southeast Asian cuisine share striking similarities in spices and flavors. Birria is a spicy, sweet, salty, and exceptionally flavorful Mexican beef stew. The meat is marinated in dried chili peppers, chipotle in adobo, vinegar, and spices, then slow-cooked until it falls apart. By combining the rich liquid from the birria preparation with chicken broth, noodles, and toppings, we birth a delightful fusion: birria taco ramen.

INGREDIENTS:

Birria:
3 ancho chili peppers
3 guajillo chili peppers
1 (7-ounce/210-g) can chipotles
   in adobo
3 tablespoons Chinkiang vinegar
   (black rice vinegar)
1 (14-ounce/400-g) can crushed
   tomatoes
2 tablespoons tomato paste
2 tablespoons light soy sauce
6 garlic cloves
2 teaspoons dried oregano
2 teaspoons smoked paprika
2 teaspoons cumin seeds or
   ground cumin

INSTRUCTIONS:

1. In a small saucepan or electric kettle, bring a few cups of water to a boil. Place the ancho and guajillo chili peppers in a large bowl, and pour the hot water over them. Let them soften for approximately 15 minutes.

2. In a blender, combine the chipotles in adobo (plus its sauce), Chinkiang, tomatoes, tomato paste, soy sauce, garlic, oregano, paprika, and cumin. Remove and discard the stems and seeds from the softened chili peppers; add the peppers to the blender. Blend until smooth.

3. Place the beef in a bowl or dish and pour the contents of the blender over it, turning to coat. Cover the beef and let marinate in the refrigerator for at least 2 hours, or preferably overnight.

4. In a large pot or Dutch oven over medium heat, warm the oil. Add the onion and sauté for 8 minutes. Add the marinated beef, bay leaves, cinnamon, and cloves. Add the broth, bring to a simmer, and then reduce

2 ¼ pounds (about 1 kg)
  beef chuck
2 tablespoons canola oil
1 yellow onion, chopped
3 bay leaves
2 cinnamon sticks
6 cloves
6 ½ cups (1 ½ liters) Mom's
  Chicken Broth (see page 127)

Pico de gallo:
3 ½ ounces (100 g) cherry
  tomatoes, chopped
½ cup (25 g) chopped cilantro
½ red onion, finely chopped
1 garlic clove, finely chopped
1 medium-hot red chili pepper,
  finely chopped
Zest and juice of 1 lime

Noodles:
8 ounces (250 g) ramen noodles,
  homemade (see page 95) or
  store-bought

Toppings:
4 small corn tortillas
7 ounces (200 g) shredded
  mozzarella cheese
4 Ajitsuke Tamago
  (see page 101)
Thinly sliced jalapeño
Thinly sliced shallots
Lime wedges (optional)

the heat to low, cover the pot, and cook and simmer for 6 hours, turning beef a few times. Remove the beef from the pot and set aside to cool (reserve the cooking liquid). When beef is cool enough to handle, shred it using two forks or your hands.

5. While the beef cooks, make the pico de gallo: in a medium bowl, combine the tomatoes, cilantro, red onion, garlic, and chili peppers. Add the lime zest and juice, and mix well.

6. Dip the tortillas in the oil formed on the surface of the broth. In a small skillet, fry one tortilla at a time over medium heat until warmed through and browned. Fill each tortilla with beef and mozzarella, and fold in half to enclose the filling.

7. In a large pot, bring a generous amount of water to a rolling boil. Add the noodles and cook until al dente. Drain thoroughly to remove as much starch as possible.

8. Divide the noodles between 4 large ramen bowls, pour over the broth, and top with the egg, jalapeño, shallots, remaining beef, and pico de gallo. Perch one filled taco on top of each bowl.

9. If desired, squeeze lime juice over the top of the ramen. Alternate between savoring the noodles and dipping the taco in the broth.

A Memory of Food

Dad's Shopping Hack

〜

My parents grew up in poverty-stricken and war-torn Vietnam. They were both the eldest in their respective sibling groups, and as such were compelled early on to contribute to the family's livelihood and manage household tasks. During the most dire times, when food was scarce, they learned that rationing and stockpiling essentials like rice and grains was vital for survival.

These challenging times left an indelible mark on my parents. Even after fleeing their homeland and settling in Sweden years ago, they retained some of these habits. Mom and Dad have always been experts in conserving and managing food. Yet, in my experience, they have never been stingy; on the contrary, they are always generous. I recall how they loved hosting friends and acquaintances, serving expansive dinners filled with an abundance of dishes.

How did two low-income individuals, without formal education, manage to support four children and yet afford to host such lavish feasts every other weekend? The secret was to buy in bulk and stock up on ingredients when they were on sale. I especially remember times when chicken was discounted. My dad had a brilliant life hack to bypass the restrictions on the maximum purchases per household. He'd take my siblings and me to the store. We'd each stand in a separate checkout lane, cash in one hand and a basket of chickens in the other. Straight into the freezer they went, and Mom had plenty of chickens to prepare her delicious broths with.

〜

NOSTALGIC NOODLES

The recipes in this chapter are my mother's noodle dishes. I grew up eating them, and they hold a special place in my heart. Every time I prepare them, I'm transported back to my childhood. Familiar aromas from the various broths permeate the kitchen and waft throughout my home.

The noodle dishes in this section need a touch of care and take a bit longer to prepare than the other noodle recipes in this book—I don't rush, but rather let each dish take the time it requires. These are perfect meals to prepare on peaceful weekends, away from the hustle and bustle of daily life. I hope that the process of making these dishes brings as much joy as eating them; perhaps some of the recipes will find a special place in your heart as well.

THANK YOU, MOM

~w~

My mother was a role model and source of inspiration throughout my upbringing, and continues to be so—not just in the realm of cooking, but in life itself. Her unwavering positivity, boundless energy, and immense patience appear inexhaustible. I am eternally grateful and happy that she is my mother. Thay, as my beloved mother is named, was born in Vietnam, and her family history stretches back to China where my grandparents were born.

As the eldest of eight children, my mother shouldered significant responsibilities from a tender age, working hard to support her family, often at the expense of her education. She was universally beloved in the neighborhood, especially among the elderly, for whom she often ran errands and did shopping.

Vietnamese markets pulsated with life and were densely populated, with stalls offering an array of fresh food including fish and meat, newly harvested vegetables, and ripe fruits. As a child, my mother relished exploring these markets. She quickly became adept at selecting the best ingredients—identifying the juiciest citrus fruits or the most flavorful tomatoes. Occasionally, she'd glean a secret ingredient from the owner of a renowned pho restaurant by observing which spices and ingredients went into their celebrated broth. This culinary intelligence formed the backbone of family meals when my grandparents were preoccupied with work.

The ingredients my mother used were simple, and so were the resulting dishes. Meat, poultry, and seafood were considered luxuries. Vegetarian meals were common, but occasionally, less-coveted parts of animals, such as pork bones or fish heads, could be procured affordably.

My mother still practices the "nose to tail" philosophy, making nourishing soups out of fish heads to accompany simple vegetable dishes with steamed rice. Some might label her a creative chef; I deem her a magician. To this day, her fish head soup remains my favorite dish, one I frequently request when I visit home. Often—to my chagrin—she declines, remarking that such a simple dish doesn't suit a celebratory homecoming.

My mother is remarkable. She fled Vietnam's oppression, poverty, and war. Arriving in Sweden, she had to cook solely from memory—it's an admirable feat. All the noodles, soups, pastries, and more she's created over the years, spanning both Chinese and Vietnamese cuisines, have greatly enriched my culinary journey. She taught me never to waste food, to always use ingredients to their utmost potential, to remain grateful for food on the table, and to remember not everyone is as fortunate. When I cook traditional dishes in my kitchen, I'm enveloped in a comforting blanket of love and warmth. Serving others the food I grew up with is my way of sharing my story and cherished childhood memories, and by extension, those of my mother as well.

Mom's Chicken Broth

Nothing can rival a rich, clear chicken broth that's been simmered patiently and lovingly. Of all the broths she made, this was the one my mother prepared most frequently. This exquisite broth requires just a few ingredients; its pristine golden hue complements virtually anything. The aroma that fills the kitchen when I make it embodies warmth and love for me.

INGREDIENTS:

1 whole chicken, ideally corn-fed
4–6 inches (10–15 cm) daikon
  radish, cut into large pieces
1 large carrot, cut into large pieces
2 yellow onions, cut into large
  pieces
2 cilantro sprigs
green onions (optional)

INSTRUCTIONS:

1. Place the chicken in a large pot and add enough water to just cover it. Bring to a boil with the lid on and let it boil for about 10 minutes, allowing foam and impurities to surface.

2. Discard the water, remove the chicken, wash out the pot, rinse the chicken, and place it back in the clean pot. Add the daikon, carrot, onions, and cilantro, and green onions, if desired. Add enough water to the pot to cover the chicken, and place over medium-high heat until the water comes to a simmer.

3. Reduce the heat to low to maintain a gentle simmer. Position two chopsticks, one on each side at the edge of the pot, before placing the lid on the pot. (This eases the pressure and simplifies monitoring the simmering.) Simmer for 3 hours.

4. Remove the chicken from the broth and set aside to cool. Strain the liquid through a fine-mesh sieve, reserving the daikon and carrots as toppings for other dishes. Remove the meat from the chicken to use for other recipes (like Spicy Chicken Noodles, page 129). Use the broth immediately, or transfer to an airtight container and refrigerate or freeze for future use. The broth remains fresh for about 5 days in the fridge and 3 months in the freezer.

Spicy Chicken Noodles

Every weekend during my childhood, my mother ensured that there were bowls of steaming broth and noodles on hand at home. This noodle dish is one she often prepared, and for me, it represents comfort. Regardless of how difficult my day may have been, this dish momentarily made me forget it all. This recipe is a tribute to my mother; I hope you will cherish it too.

INGREDIENTS:

2 ½ cups (600 ml) Mom's Chicken
   Broth (see page 127)
MSG
Salt
1 ¼ cups (275 g) bean sprouts
4 ounces (125 g) rice noodles
½ cup (65 g) shredded chicken
   (see page 127)
2 tablespoons Crispy Shallot Oil
   (see page 28)
¼ cup (26 g) finely chopped green
   onions
¼ cup (12 g) finely chopped cilantro
Freshly ground black pepper

Sauce:
1 tablespoon toasted sesame oil
2 tablespoons light soy sauce
1 tablespoon Chinkiang vinegar
   (black rice vinegar)
2 tablespoons Crispy Chili Oil
   (see page 29)

INSTRUCTIONS:

1. In a medium pot over medium heat, warm the broth and season with MSG and salt to taste. Reduce the heat to low to keep the broth warm.

2. Bring a small pot of water to a boil, add the bean sprouts, and boil for 1 minute. Drain and set aside.

3. Make the sauce: in a small bowl, combine the sesame oil, soy sauce, Chinkiang, and chili oil.

4. Place the noodles in a large bowl. Boil a generous amount of water and pour it over the noodles (there should be enough water to cover the noodles), then cover the bowl. Let the noodles sit for 10–15 minutes, occasionally lifting the lid to gently separate the noodles if they are sticking together. Taste a noodle or two as they begin to soften: you'll know they are done when they're flexible enough to wind around your finger and they have a pleasant al dente bite. Drain the noodles and rinse with cold water.

5. Divide the noodles between 2 bowls, and top with bean sprouts and chicken. Pour the steaming broth over the noodles. Top each bowl with 3 tablespoons sauce, 1 tablespoon shallot oil, half the green onions and cilantro, and a generous amount of pepper.

Wontons with Egg Noodles

From a young age, I assisted my mother in the kitchen by folding wontons whenever this dish was to be served. Wontons with egg noodles is a classic Cantonese noodle dish, and one I grew up with. Silky wontons in a steaming chicken broth with egg noodles and simple accompaniments will humble anyone from the very first slurp.

INGREDIENTS:

3 ⅓ cups (800 ml) Mom's Chicken Broth (see page 127)
MSG
Salt
1 head bok choy
¾ cup (175 g) bean sprouts
10 filled wontons (see page 71)
4 ounces (180 g) egg noodles
½ cup (25 g) finely chopped cilantro
½ cup (70 g) finely chopped green onions
2 tablespoons Crispy Shallot Oil (see page 28)
Freshly ground black pepper

Sauce:
4 tablespoons Crispy Chili Oil (see page 29)
3 tablespoons light soy sauce
1 tablespoon toasted sesame oil
2 tablespoons Chinkiang vinegar (black rice vinegar)

INSTRUCTIONS:

1. In a medium pot over medium heat, warm the broth and season with a pinch each of MSG and salt. Reduce the heat to low to keep the broth warm.

2. Make the sauce: in a small bowl, combine the chili oil, soy sauce, sesame oil, and Chinkiang.

3. Separate the bok choy into leaves. Bring a medium pot of water to a boil, add the bok choy leaves and bean sprouts, and boil for 1 minute. Drain and set aside.

4. In a large pot, bring a generous amount of water to a rolling boil, ensuring there's ample room for the wontons to move around. Add the wontons and let boil until they float to the surface, 4–5 minutes. Remove them from the pot using a slotted spoon and transfer to a plate or bowl.

5. In the same pot of water, cook the noodles as per the package instructions or until al dente. Drain.

6. Divide the noodles and wontons between 2 bowls and pour the broth over them. Top each bowl with bok choy, bean sprouts, 2 tablespoons sauce, cilantro, green onions, shallot oil, and pepper to taste.

7. Serve the remaining sauce in smaller bowls to use as a dip for the wontons.

Mom's Pho

Pho, Vietnam's national dish, is adored by many. Despite its clear broth, it's surprisingly aromatic and rich with flavors from spices like cinnamon, star anise, and cardamom. Paired with rice noodles, beef, and especially an abundance of fresh herbs, the dish becomes addictively delicious, making you yearn for more after each slurp. One should never underestimate Mom's pho!

Beef bones and marrow bones are available in most grocery stores (often frozen), at meat counters, and in markets. Beef meatballs are used as toppings for pho. If you don't want to make them yourself, you can find them in the frozen section of Asian stores.

As in the Beef Chow Fun recipe (page 61), it's easiest to slice the beef if it's semi-frozen, so I recommend you plan ahead and place the ribeye in the freezer for two hours before working with it.

INGREDIENTS:

3 cinnamon sticks
3 star anise pods
4 bay leaves
1 tablespoon cumin seeds
4 whole green cardamom pods
½ tablespoon black peppercorns
½ tablespoon fennel seeds
2-inch (5-cm) piece ginger, peeled and split lengthwise
1 large yellow onion, peeled and halved
2 ¼ pounds (1 kg) beef marrow bones (or soup bones)
2 ¼ pounds (1 kg) beef bones
1 pound (500 g) beef chuck
4–6 inches (10–15 cm) radish, in thick slices
5 tablespoons fish sauce
2 tablespoons granulated sugar
1 teaspoon MSG

INSTRUCTIONS:

1. In a large dry skillet over medium-high heat, toast the cinnamon sticks, star anise, bay leaves, cumin, cardamom, peppercorns, and fennel seeds for 2 minutes. Transfer toasted spices to a bowl. In the same skillet over medium-high heat, toast the cut sides of the ginger and onion, checking them occasionally, until they are slightly charred around the edges. Remove to a plate and set aside.

2. Rinse the marrow bones, beef bones, and beef chuck under running water. Place them in a large pot with at least a 1 ½ gallon (6-liter) capacity. Add enough water to just cover the contents, bring to a boil, and let simmer for 10 minutes. Remove the chuck, marrow bones, and beef bones from the pot and rinse off the foam. Wash out the pot.

3. Return the meat, marrow, and bones to the clean pot along with the toasted spices, ginger, onion, and radish. Fill the pot with water so that it just covers the contents, and place over medium-high heat until it comes to a simmer.

4. Reduce the heat to low to maintain a gentle simmer. Position two chopsticks, one on each side at the edge of the pot, before placing the lid on the pot. (This eases the pressure and simplifies monitoring the simmering.) Simmer for 3 hours.

Accompaniments and topping:
12 beef meatballs, thawed if frozen
10 ½ ounces (300 g) ribeye steak, preferably semi-frozen
1 cup (220 g) bean sprouts
12 ounces (540 g) wide rice noodles
½ yellow onion, thinly sliced
½ cup (25 g) finely chopped culantro (Mexican cilantro)
½ cup (25 g) finely chopped cilantro
½ cup (70 g) finely chopped green onions
1 large medium-hot red chili pepper, seeds removed, sliced
1 cup (48 g) Thai basil leaves
6 tablespoons hoisin sauce, plus more for serving
Freshly ground black pepper
Lime wedges, for garnish
Sriracha (optional), for garnish

5. Remove the beef chuck from the pot and place it on a plate; it should now be tender and flavorful. Allow it to cool, then wrap it in plastic wrap and refrigerate for another use. Let the broth simmer for another hour. Strain the broth and add the fish sauce, sugar, and MSG. The broth should be aromatic and balanced, tasting of beef with just a hint of sweetness. Add the beef meatballs to the broth and keep it warm over low heat.

6. Slice the ribeye very thinly.

7. Bring a medium pot of water to a boil, add the bean sprouts, and boil for 1 minute. Drain and set aside.

8. Place the noodles in a large bowl. Boil a generous amount of water and pour it over the noodles (there should be enough water to cover the noodles), then cover the bowl. Let the noodles sit for 10–15 minutes, occasionally lifting the lid to gently separate the noodles if they are sticking together. Taste a noodle or two as they begin to soften: you'll know they are done when they're flexible enough to wind around your finger and they have a pleasant al dente bite. Drain the noodles and rinse with cold water.

9. Divide the noodles between 6 bowls. Add the sliced ribeye and pour the piping hot broth over to cook the meat. Top each bowl with meatballs, bean sprouts, sliced onions, culantro, cilantro, green onions, chili peppers, Thai basil, 1 tablespoon hoisin sauce, and pepper, to taste. Serve with lime wedges to squeeze over the top and hoisin and sriracha to dip the meat into.

Bun Rieu

When most people think of Vietnamese noodle dishes, pho is what comes to mind. This is understandable given its popularity and its prevalence in Vietnamese restaurants. However, allow me to introduce you to a lesser-known Vietnamese noodle dish that I guarantee will satisfy your taste buds. Bun rieu is a chicken-broth-based dish brimming with tomatoes and deep seafood flavors. The combination of chicken and seafood might be unusual, but I promise almost everyone who tries it loves it. Pho, watch out—there's a new sheriff in town.

INGREDIENTS:

Broth:
½ cup (120 g) dried mini shrimp
3 tablespoons canola oil
4 tomatoes, coarsely chopped
2 tablespoons tomato paste
½ teaspoon salt
½ teaspoon granulated sugar
6 cups (1 ½ liters) Mom's Chicken
  Broth (see page 127)
4 tablespoons tamarind paste
½ cube fish bouillon
4 tablespoons shrimp paste
  in bean oil
3 large eggs

Accompaniments and toppings:
2 cups (180 g) bean sprouts
3 ½ ounces (100 g) fried tofu
8 ounces (250 g) rice noodles
9 ounces (250 g) Vietnamese
  salami, sliced
½ cup (70 g) finely chopped
  green onions
½ cup (25 g) finely chopped cilantro
Thai basil leaves, for garnish
4 tablespoons Crispy Shallot Oil
  (see page 28)
3 celery stalks, shaved lengthwise
  with a vegetable peeler
4 tablespoons fish sauce
Lime wedges, for garnish

INSTRUCTIONS:

1. Fill a medium bowl with water and the tomatoes, add the shrimp, and let soak for 45 minutes.

2. In a 2-quart (2-l) pot over medium-high heat, warm the canola oil over medium-high heat. Remove the shrimp from the water and add it and tomatoes to the pot and sauté for 2 minutes. Stir in the tomato paste, salt, and sugar and sauté for another 2 minutes. Add the broth and bring to a simmer. Add the tamarind paste and fish bouillon and continue to simmer.

3. In a medium bowl, whisk together the shrimp paste and eggs. Ensure the broth is simmering, not boiling, then gently pour in the egg mixture.

4. Bring a medium pot of water to a boil, add the bean sprouts, and boil for 1 minute. Drain and set aside.

5. Cut the tofu into bite-sized pieces, if necessary, and add to the broth.

6. Place the noodles in a large bowl. Boil a generous amount of water and pour it over the noodles (there should be enough water to cover the noodles), then cover the bowl. Let the noodles sit for 10–15 minutes, occasionally lifting the lid to gently separate the noodles if they are sticking together. Taste a noodle or two as they begin to soften: you'll know they are done when they're flexible enough to wind around your finger and they have a pleasant al dente bite. Drain the noodles and rinse with cold water.

7. Divide the noodles between 4 bowls. Add the broth containing the eggs and tofu. Top each bowl with bean sprouts, salami, green onions, cilantro, Thai basil, 1 tablespoon shallot oil, and shaved celery. Finish each bowl with 1 tablespoon fish sauce, and squeeze a lime wedge into each bowl.

Bun Bo Hue

Bun bo Hue, much like bun rieu, is a somewhat overlooked noodle dish from the city of Hue in Vietnam. The soup takes on an orange-red hue tint to the generous amount of saté sauce. Unlike pho, Bun bo Hue is made with both pork and beef. The flavors of lemongrass, fish sauce, shrimp paste, and lime leaves make the soup complex and flavorful. Could Bun bo hue become a new favorite?

The specific cuts of meat used in this recipe can be found frozen in most grocery stores, or fresh at meat counters. Lime leaves can be found frozen in most Asian stores.

INGREDIENTS:

Broth:
1 ½ pounds (750 g) pork bones
1 pound (500 g) oxtail
¾ pound (375 g) beef brisket
4 lemongrass stalks
1 yellow onion, halved
4 garlic cloves, lightly crushed
1-inch (2 1/2-cm) piece ginger,
  peeled and cut into 4 slices
1 tablespoon red pepper flakes
2 star anise pods
5 lime leaves
2 tablespoons shrimp paste
  in bean oil
4 tablespoons fish sauce
2 tablespoons brown sugar
  or granulated sugar
Salt

Accompaniments and toppings:
1 handful bean sprouts
8 ounces (250 g) rice noodles
½ Vietnamese salami, sliced
4 tablespoons Saté Sauce
  (see page 26)
½ cup (70 g) finely chopped
  green onions
½ cup (25 g) finely chopped
  cilantro
Thai basil leaves
1 chili pepper, sliced
Lime wedges

INSTRUCTIONS:

1. Make the broth: in a large pot, combine the bones, oxtail, and brisket. Add enough water to just cover the contents, bring to a boil, and reduce heat to low. Let simmer for 15 minutes, until foam forms on the surface. Remove the bones and meat from the pot and rinse off the foam. Wash out the pot, and return the bones and meat to the clean pot.

2. Remove the outermost layer from the lemongrass stalks and pound them using the handle of a knife to release aromatic oils. Cut in half crosswise.

3. In a large dry skillet over medium-high heat, toast the lemongrass, onion, garlic, ginger, red pepper flakes, and star anise. Once the onion starts charring slightly, transfer the skillet's ingredients to the pot with the meat and bones. Add the lime leaves, shrimp paste, fish sauce, and sugar. Add enough water to the pot to just cover the contents, and place over medium-high heat until it comes to a simmer.

4. Reduce the heat to low to maintain a gentle simmer. Position two chopsticks, one on each side at the edge of the pot, before placing the lid on the pot. (This eases the pressure and simplifies monitoring the simmering.) Simmer for 3 hours.

5. Remove the meat and bones from the pot. Set the brisket aside on a plate and let cool, then cut into slices. Discard bones and oxtail.

6. Strain the broth through a fine sieve to get a clear broth. Season with salt to taste (or add more fish sauce if you prefer more saltiness).

7. Bring a medium pot of water to a boil, add the bean sprouts, and boil for 1 minute. Drain and set aside.

8. Place the noodles in a large bowl. Boil a generous amount of water and pour it over the noodles (there should be enough water to cover the noodles), then cover the bowl. Let the noodles sit for 10–15 minutes, occasionally lifting the lid to gently separate the noodles if they are sticking together. Taste a noodle or two as they begin to soften: you'll know they are done when they're flexible enough to wind around your finger and they have a pleasant al dente bite. Drain the noodles and rinse with cold water.

9. Divide the noodles between 4 bowls and add slices of brisket and salami. Pour the hot broth over and garnish each bowl with 1 tablespoon saté sauce, green onions, cilantro, Thai basil, bean sprouts, and sliced chili peppers, and a squeezed lime wedge.

Bo Kho (Mom's Beef Stew)

When my mother prepared this dish, it was usually wintertime. There was nothing quite like returning home, stepping into warmth after playing in the snow, completely cold and famished, only to be greeted by the delightful aroma of bo kho. Mom always made a large batch that lasted nearly a week for our family of six. The brilliance of this dish is its versatility. Initially, it can be enjoyed as a stew: with a somewhat thicker consistency, eaten with a spoon. Later, diluted with chicken broth, a bit more seasoning, noodles, and fresh herbs, it transforms into a soup.

INGREDIENTS:

Meat:
1 ¾ pound (800 g) chuck roast or similar cut
2 garlic cloves, pressed
3 tablespoons grated ginger
5 tablespoons fish sauce
2 ½ teaspoons five-spice powder
½ tablespoon brown sugar or granulated sugar

Broth:
3 stalks lemongrass
3 tablespoons canola oil
6 garlic cloves, finely chopped
1 yellow onion, sliced
4 tablespoons tomato paste
2 ¼ quarts (2 l) chicken broth
1 2/3 cups (400 ml) coconut water
2 star anise pods
2 bay leaves
1 cinnamon stick
1 teaspoon freshly ground black pepper
1 teaspoon chili powder
1 tablespoon paprika
6 carrots, cut into 4/5-inch (2-cm) slices
1 teaspoon salt
1 tablespoon light soy sauce
3 tablespoons Crispy Chili Oil (see page 29)

Accompaniments and toppings:
8 ounces (250 g) wide rice noodles
½ cup (25 g) finely chopped cilantro
½ cup (25 g) Thai basil leaves
1 yellow onion, thinly sliced
Lime wedges
Fish sauce

INSTRUCTIONS:

1. Prepare the meat: cut the chuck roast into 1 ½ -inch (4 cm) cubes. Place in a large bowl and add the garlic, ginger, fish sauce, five-spice powder, and sugar. Toss to coat, and then set aside to marinate for 30 minutes.

2. Make the broth: cut one stalk of lemongrass in half crosswise and lightly tap the halves with the handle of a knife to release their aromatic oils. Remove the outer layer of the other lemongrass stalks, cut off and discard the hard root at the bottom, and finely chop the remaining lemongrass.

3. In a large pot (at least 1 ½ gallon/6-l capacity) over medium-high heat, warm the canola oil. Add the halved lemongrass to the pot and sauté for 1 minute. Reduce the heat to medium, add the chopped lemongrass and garlic, and sauté for an additional 2 minutes.

4. Add the onion and sauté until it softens and starts to become translucent. Increase the heat to medium-high and add the marinated meat, turning to brown it on all sides. Add the tomato paste, stir to incorporate, and sauté for 5 minutes.

5. Pour in the chicken broth and coconut water and add the star anise, bay leaves, cinnamon stick, pepper, chili powder, and paprika. Reduce the heat to low and allow the mixture to simmer, covered, for 2 hours.

6. Add the carrots, salt, soy sauce, and chili oil. Continue to simmer for 40 minutes.

7. Place the noodles in a large bowl. Boil a generous amount of water and pour it over the noodles (there should be enough water to cover the noodles), then cover the bowl. Let the noodles sit for 10–15 minutes, occasionally lifting the lid to gently separate the noodles if they are sticking together. Taste a noodle or two as they begin to soften: you'll know they are done when they're flexible enough to wind around your finger and they have a pleasant al dente bite. Drain the noodles and rinse with cold water.

8. Divide the noodles between 4 bowls. Ladle the soup over them, removing the bay leaves, star anise, cinnamon stick, and large lemongrass pieces if spotted. Top with cilantro, Thai basil, and onions. Adjust the flavor with lime juice and fish sauce to find the perfect balance between saltiness and acidity.

Khao Soi

Khao soi is a rich and delicious noodle dish with coconut and curry. It originated from the Yunnan province in China as a broth-based curry; the coconut cream was introduced when the Dai people brought the dish to northern Thailand. Today, khao soi stands as the most iconic curry in Chiang Mai, and is also immensely popular in neighboring countries Myanmar and Laos. It boasts an incredibly hearty and flavorful profile that is sure to delight your taste buds.

INGREDIENTS:

Broth:
2 tablespoons canola oil
2 garlic cloves, finely chopped
1 tablespoon finely chopped ginger
1 tablespoon tomato paste
4 tablespoons red curry paste
4 ¼ cups (1 l) Mom's Chicken Broth (see page 127)
3 cups (720 ml) coconut milk
½ puck palm sugar
4 tablespoons fish sauce

Accompaniments and toppings:
2 green onions
3 large eggs
Canola oil, for frying
5 wonton wrappers
8 ounces (250 g) egg noodles
1 cup (65 g) shredded chicken (see Mom's Chicken Broth, page 127)
1 shallot, sliced
Lime wedges

INSTRUCTIONS:

1. In a pot with a 2–3 liter (2–3 quart) capacity over medium heat, warm the canola oil. Add the garlic and ginger and sauté for 1 minute to release their aromas.

2. Add the tomato paste and red curry paste. Sauté for 3 minutes, until the oil takes on a reddish hue.

3. Increase the heat to medium-high, add the broth and coconut milk, and bring to a boil. Reduce the heat to medium-low to attain a gentle simmer.

4. Add the sugar and fish sauce, stirring until the sugar dissolves. Adjust the seasoning, adding more fish sauce for saltiness and sugar for sweetness. Set the broth aside.

5. Cut the green onions in half crosswise and then slice them thinly lengthwise. Transfer to a medium bowl, cover with cold water, and let them soak until serving.

6. In a medium bowl, whisk the eggs. In a small nonstick skillet over low heat, pour in a thin layer of the eggs and let sit until cooked through into a thin pancake. Transfer the egg to a plate. Repeat until all the egg mixture has been used. Once all eggs are cooked, roll up the pancakes and slice them into 1/8-inch (3-mm) strips. Set aside.

7. In a large pot over medium-high heat, heat the canola oil to 320°F (160°C). The oil should fill the pot about 1/3 of the way. If you don't have a thermometer, you can test the oil by dipping a dry wooden chopstick into it: if the oil bubbles around the chopstick, it's hot enough.

8. Slice the wonton wrappers into 1/5-inch (5-mm) wide strips and carefully fry in batches until golden, removing them from the oil using a slotted spoon or small strainer and transferring them to paper towels to drain.

9. Cook the noodles as per the package instructions or until al dente. Drain and rinse with cold water.

10. Reheat the broth if necessary. Divide the noodles between 4 bowls, pour in the broth, and top with chicken, egg strips, wonton strips, shallot, green onions, and a lime wedge. If desired, add more fish sauce for additional saltiness.

Laksa

The first time I tasted this spicy Singaporean noodle soup called laksa was at a quaint family-owned restaurant in China with just ten seats. My family members and I each ordered a bowl, and upon savoring its deep and intense flavors, I was immediately enthralled.

INGREDIENTS:

Broth:
2 tablespoons canola oil
2 garlic cloves, finely chopped
1 tablespoon finely chopped ginger
1 small hot red chili pepper, finely chopped
1 lemongrass stalk, hard root discarded, finely chopped
2 tablespoons laksa paste
1 tablespoon brown sugar or granulated sugar
4 ¼ cups (1 l) Mom's Chicken Broth (see page 127)
3 cups (700 ml) coconut milk
2 tablespoons fish sauce
3 ½ ounces (100 g) fried tofu,
Juice of 1 lime
1 tablespoon sriracha
2 tablespoons Crispy Chili Oil (see page 29)

Accompaniments and toppings:
8 raw shrimp (or prawns), rinsed, peeled, and deveined
Salt and freshly ground black pepper
2 tablespoons canola oil
1 cup (220 g) bean sprouts
8 ounces (250 g) thin rice noodles
1 cup (130 g) shredded chicken (see page 127)
1/4 cup (12 g) finely chopped cilantro
4 tablespoons Crispy Shallot Oil (see page 28)
Lime wedges

INSTRUCTIONS:

1. In a large pot over medium heat, warm the canola oil. Add the garlic and ginger and sauté for 1 minute. Add the chili pepper and lemongrass and sauté for 3 minutes. Add the laksa paste and sugar, sautéing until all the aromas are released, about 3 minutes.

2. Add the broth, coconut milk, fish sauce, and tofu. Bring to a simmer and cook for 10 minutes. Add the lime juice, sriracha, and chili oil. Taste and adjust seasonings.

3. Season the shrimp with 2 pinches each salt and pepper. In a large skillet over medium-high heat, warm the canola oil and quickly sauté the shrimp, about 30 seconds per side. Transfer to a plate.

4. Bring a medium pot of water to a boil, add the bean sprouts, and boil for 1 minute. Drain and set aside.

5. Place the noodles in a large bowl. Boil a generous amount of water and pour it over the noodles (there should be enough water to cover the noodles), then cover the bowl. Let the noodles sit for 10–15 minutes, occasionally lifting the lid to gently separate the noodles if they are sticking together. Taste a noodle or two as they begin to soften: you'll know they are done when they're flexible enough to wind around your finger and they have a pleasant al dente bite. Drain the noodles and rinse with cold water.

6. Divide the noodles between 4 bowls. Top with bean sprouts and chicken. Add the soup with its tofu, and then garnish each bowl with shrimp, cilantro, 1 tablespoon of shallot oil, and lime juice.

Memories of Food

Cooking on the Sly

When I was a child, my parents set many clear boundaries, but one in particular stood out: we children were never to use the stove when no adult was home. Despite that, when my parents were away, my ten-year-old brother and I (age seven) would sneakily disobey this rule.

Our combined culinary expertise extended to a rotating menu of three dishes: toasted sandwiches, boxed macaroni and cheese with ham, and instant noodles. Of course, there was always food prepared by our mother, ready to be warmed up, but on some days, the mac and cheese seemed more appealing than the grilled duck in the fridge. Because we knew our actions were strictly forbidden, we made sure to eat quickly and then air out the house. We cleaned as if wiping away evidence from a crime scene.

~~~

Now, as I sit at my kitchen table, I can hardly believe I'm penning the concluding words of a book I never imagined I'd write. Looking back at my initial meeting with my publisher, the realization of having a finished book fills me with immense joy and pride. One thing's certain—I couldn't have done this alone, and I'd like to deeply thank a few special individuals:

My partner Sara (who's also the designer of this beautiful book) for being my best friend and ever-present support, constantly providing feedback and enduring the persistent cooking noises of sizzling food and whirring fans. I'm thrilled to have you on this journey. Our dog Alfons, always by my side in the kitchen, offering affectionate kisses and dragging me out for walks when most needed. I love you both. My dear parents, Thay and Sanh, for your unconditional love, nurturing upbringing, and the wondrous meals from my childhood; it's from you that my love for food originates. My siblings Joakim, Emmy, and Mikael, for giving me an upbringing second to none. Your unwavering support and cherished memories mean the world to me. Thank you for letting me be your younger brother—I love you.

My incredible publisher, Gunilla Bergmark, for your warmth, encouragement, and above all, your faith in me. My photographer, Lina Eidenberg Adamo, for always being available and for the stunning photos—it's been comforting having you on this project. My editor, Maria Selin, for your dedication, patience, and positivity. You consistently teach me new things, and offer invaluable insights and suggestions. And of course, a heartfelt thanks to the rest of the team for your commitment and support.

Lastly, I'd like to express my gratitude to Markus Mauritzson for the loan of porcelain and Thomas Lyon for your beautiful creations. My dear friend Julia Tuvesson, for your unwavering encouragement and belief that anything is possible. My extended family and cherished friends, thank you for your continuous support and for always being there. I'm truly grateful for each one of you.

INDEX

SLURP: RECIPES TO ELEVATE YOUR NOODLES

Author
Dennis Yen

U.S. Edition Publisher & Creative Director
Ilona Oppenheim

U.S. Edition Art Director & Cover Design
Jefferson Quintana

U.S. Edition Typesetter
Leonardo van Schermbeek

U.S. Edition Editorial Director
Lisa McGuinness

U.S. Edition Editorial Coordinator
Jessica Faroy

Printed and bound in China by Shenzhen Reliance Printers.

ISBN: 978-1-962098-10-6

Slurp: Recipes to Elevate Your Noodles is printed on Forest
Stewardship Council-certified paper from well-managed forests.

Tra Publishing is committed to sustainability in its materials and practices.

Tra Publishing
245 NE 37th Street
Miami, FL 33137
trapublishing.com

T tra.publishing

1 2 3 4 5 6 7 8 9 10